THRIVING TOGETHER

Praise for *Thriving Together*

This book is a must-read for all educators who seek to create a culture of wellbeing in schools. David Kolpak shares his expertise on embedding the science and practice of wellbeing. An innovative school leader and educator for three decades and a leader in the field of wellbeing education, he has so much to share with us.

– Professor Lea Waters AM, PhD, psychologist, researcher and positive education expert

Filled with evidence-based information and the latest research, David's book is an important resource. It will assist schools and their leadership to develop a best-practice framework to embed a wellbeing focus across their school community. I highly recommend this book, which should become a vital addition to every educator and school leader's professional library.

– Susan McLean, Director, Cyber Safety Solutions

This book is a testament to David's deep experience as an educator and his unwavering passion for wellbeing. Drawing from over 30 years of practice, David offers a compelling and practical guide for fostering flourishing school communities. His insights are not only grounded in research but enriched by his real-world understanding of what educators and students need to thrive. David's credibility and genuine dedication to wellbeing shine through on every page.

– Ash Manuel, Founder, Growing With Gratitude

David Kolpak is a visionary educational leader whose innovative wellbeing approach has transformed countless schools and lives. This book is a powerful and practical guide that encapsulates David's wealth of experience, offering educators a clear roadmap to embed wellbeing at every level of school life.

– Chris Ramsden, Educational Consultant at Accelium and Mind Lab Australia

As a school leader I have long admired David's genuine commitment to wellbeing and the way he has so successfully embedded this in schools. How fortunate are we to now have this practical, easily adaptable resource backed up by research, science and over 30 years of experience in a variety of educational settings.

– John Robinson, Principal, Investigator College

An essential resource for any educator or school leader committed to embedding wellbeing across their school community. Backed by the latest research and practical experience, this book provides adaptable, evidence-based strategies that can be seamlessly integrated into classrooms, staffrooms and leadership practice.

– Ben Storer, Deputy Head of Junior School, Wellbeing and Administration, St Peter's College

A thoughtful and practical guide for anyone looking to grow in the wellbeing space, not only for educators wanting to enhance their own practice but also for school leaders striving to create meaningful whole-school change.

– Christopher Clausen, Teacher, Trinity College North

THRIVING TOGETHER

A Blueprint for Flourishing Staff and Students

David Kolpak

Published in 2025 by Amba Press, Melbourne, Australia
www.ambapress.com.au

© David Kolpak 2025

All rights reserved. No part of this book may be reproduced or transmitted in any form or by any means, electronic or mechanical, including photocopying, recording or by any information storage and retrieval system, without prior permission in writing from the publisher.

Cover design: Tess McCabe
Internal design: Amba Press
Editor: Brooke Lyons

ISBN: 9781923215641 (pbk)
ISBN: 9781923215658 (ebk)

A catalogue record for this book is available from the National Library of Australia.

CONTENTS

Foreword		vii
Introduction		1
Chapter 1	Teaching Wellbeing	5
Chapter 2	Speaking the Language of Wellbeing	25
Chapter 3	Inspiring Trust and Growth	43
Chapter 4	Flourishing Through Purpose and Forgiveness	61
Chapter 5	Planning a Whole-School Approach	77
Chapter 6	Implementing a Whole-School Approach	93
Chapter 7	Unstoppable Growth	111
Chapter 8	Supercharging Student Wellbeing	129
Chapter 9	Creating a Trauma-Informed Classroom	145
Chapter 10	Unlocking Wellbeing	159
Afterword: Unlocking the Path to Wellbeing		177
Resources		179
References		183
Acknowledgements		187
About the Author		189

FOREWORD

In the ever-evolving landscape of education, where the demands on educators grow more intricate with each passing year, the importance of wellbeing – both personal and collective – has never been more pressing. Teaching is more than a profession; it is a calling, a journey of heart and intellect, where the impact on young minds shapes not just the present, but the future. Yet, in the noble pursuit of nurturing others, educators often overlook their own needs, leaving them vulnerable to burnout and disengagement.

This book, authored by an exceptional and seasoned Principal, serves as a timely and invaluable guide for fostering educator and student wellbeing, and cultivating a school culture grounded in care, connection and resilience. Drawing from years of frontline leadership, Kolpak's insights resonate with authenticity, wisdom and a deep understanding of the challenges and opportunities within our schools.

Thriving Together offers practical strategies for educators to prioritise their own mental, emotional and physical health, while also illuminating the pathway for leaders and school communities to embed wellbeing into the very fabric of their culture.

The examples within these pages are both compelling and relatable. They remind us that wellbeing is not a one-size-fits-all endeavour, but a nuanced and dynamic process that requires intentionality, empathy and collaboration. From addressing the unique stressors of the teaching profession to building systems of peer support and professional development, this book provides a blueprint for sustainable change.

As someone who has witnessed the transformative power of wellbeing in schools, I can attest to the profound ripple effects it creates. When educators are cared for, they are better equipped to care for their students.

When school cultures prioritise respect, trust and balance, everyone – from staff to students to families – benefits. This book reminds us that wellbeing is not a luxury; it is a foundation for excellence.

Whether you are a teacher seeking tools to enhance your own wellbeing, a school leader committed to creating a positive culture, or an advocate for systemic change in education, this book will leave you inspired and empowered. It is a call to action, a source of hope, and a testament to what is possible when we place wellbeing at the heart of our schools.

I am honoured to introduce this remarkable work and invite you to embark on this journey of transformation. May it serve as a beacon for educators everywhere, lighting the way toward healthier, happier and more vibrant school communities.

Madhavi Nawana Parker
Managing Director, Positive Minds Australia

INTRODUCTION

When I first began my journey as Deputy Head of Junior School at a leading college in South Australia, my focus was primarily on managing student behaviour. I was the person students had to see every time they behaved poorly. My job was to work with students so they would learn not to make the same mistakes again. In the beginning I was primarily working from a deficit model.

However, as I continued to learn and grow, my perspective shifted towards understanding the broader concept of student wellbeing. I realised that behaviour isn't something that needs to be managed; instead, it is a reflection of a student's overall wellbeing. This change in outlook was profound, and it led me to explore the many facets of nurturing and supporting students in a holistic way.

I would often hear the words 'What's wrong with you?' when students were being 'dealt with' by teachers. But it wasn't long before a new way of speaking and a new approach guided me towards changing this language. It was time instead to focus on 'What's right with you?'

Positive psychology played a significant role in this transformation by allowing me to adopt a more proactive rather than reactive approach. By focusing on cultivating students' strengths, emotional intelligence and resilience, I encouraged them to flourish in all aspects of life. This shift towards a more positive, strengths-based approach opened up new possibilities for creating supportive and enriching environments where students could truly thrive.

My passion to find ways of combating the ever-increasing challenges of mental ill-health facing our young people saw me undertake further learning to grow my knowledge, understanding and skills to be able to connect with the students.

I was blessed to work with a team of people who saw my strengths in this area and supported my growth (see the Acknowledgements section at the back of this book for further details). I tried, I experimented, I succeeded and I made mistakes; but all the while I was learning that for students and schools to be successful in the wellbeing space, they needed to be flexible, adaptable and have an agile approach to meet the needs of the students.

My first real 'aha' moment came via the training I received from the University of Pennsylvania – the Penn Resiliency Program. Over six days I, and a number of my colleagues, were taken through an evidence-based program aimed at developing skills in resilience. As a teacher, I approached this learning anticipating the end result to be a program to deliver to my students. Instead, what I discovered was that the entire week was more about me developing as a human – learning to understand myself, my thinking patterns, my relationships, my communication style and my strengths so that I could be the best version of myself. I had to learn to know, value and love myself so that when I engaged in my home or school environment, those around me would receive the most authentic version of me possible. And that's the point where more questions started:

- *How do we make our school environments a place where staff and students were able to be the best version of themselves?*
- *How do we create opportunities for school communities to thrive?*
- *What would our schools be like if their members experienced significant periods of flow (a state of deep focus, enjoyment and optimal performance)?*
- *How can we make a school environment a place where relationships are fundamental to creating deep connections with ourselves and each other?*
- *What do we need to do to create a common language that we all speak based on our context?*

I have now had over 30 years' experience in education. I have had the privilege of working with students aged three to 16 years and have served as a classroom teacher, specialist teacher, Curriculum Coordinator, Head of House, Deputy Head, Wellbeing Leader and Principal. These roles have allowed me to witness first-hand the diverse needs of students and the positive impact of effective wellbeing practices. I understand clearly that there is a significant difference between wellbeing and happiness, and that as educators we need to be clear about the distinction. By combining these experiences with the insights and learnings from the extraordinary individuals I have been fortunate enough to meet, work or present with, I have been able to refine my craft and develop strategies that truly reach and assist students to develop their toolkits to flourish.

Throughout my journey, I have been blessed to work with and be inspired by a range of remarkable individuals whose contributions have shaped my understanding of wellbeing and education. Each of these people has brought unique insights and expertise that have left a lasting impact on both my personal and professional growth. Their work has guided me in deepening my knowledge and embracing new approaches to fostering wellbeing for students, staff and communities alike.

As you explore this book, I hope you find yourself inspired by the work of these and other outstanding thinkers I mention in the book. Their influence on my journey has been profound, and I believe their insights will resonate with you as you embark on your own path towards greater wellbeing and fulfillment.

With warmth and gratitude,
David

Navigating this book

It's important to remember that wellbeing and wellbeing frameworks are not always linear or sequential. Their parts are woven together and are enacted at different times for different reasons. Therefore, this book has been written to demonstrate many of the facets of wellbeing and how they all interact with each other. It will take you through:

- **Guiding wellbeing as a whole-school strategy:** this is key to embedding wellbeing into the culture with a shared vision and intentional planning.
- **Supercharging wellbeing with responsive strategies:** making small shifts in how we respond to students – whether through creating safe spaces, encouraging service learning or building social-emotional connections.
- **Unlocking wellbeing for lasting success:** to sustain momentum, align wellbeing strategies with educational standards and embrace frameworks that emphasise growth, connection and hope.

- **Inspiring staff trust and growth:** building trust, fostering connection, creating a strengths-based feedback culture and empowering staff to thrive.
- **Flourishing through purpose and forgiveness:** staff create a clear path forward, reconnecting with their 'why' and cultivating practices that allow them to maintain focus and balance.
- **Speaking the language of wellbeing:** creating a shared understanding and clear definitions to lay the foundation for a cohesive, supportive culture.
- **Teaching resilience in context:** wellbeing is not just about happiness – it's about resilience, adaptability and context, and tailoring strategies to meet the diverse needs of staff and students.
- **Enhancing culture through gratitude and nature:** gratitude and connection to nature fosters a sense of belonging and connection for students and staff.
- **Creating a trauma-informed classroom:** cultivating flourishing classrooms that are safe, inclusive spaces for all.
- **Unlocking unstoppable growth:** building student capacity, resilience, agency and grit through intentional teaching, modelling and opportunities for growth.

CHAPTER 1
TEACHING WELLBEING
Resilience in Context

Discover the essence of wellbeing and the importance of teaching it. Uncover why context matters and how tailored wellbeing programs emphasise the power of resilience.

Wellbeing! It's a term we've all heard and spoken a lot. It seems as though every time we turn on our television or radio we hear about something that is good for our wellbeing. From fitness and healthcare products, to mental health and wellness apps, to personal care and beauty products, to healthy eating and drinking remedies, to wellness retreats and experiences, to banking and financial services, to medical and health-related interventions. All of these will claim to target a specific part of our life and provide benefit to our wellbeing. But when we use the word 'wellbeing', what are we actually meaning?

What does wellbeing even mean?

Wellbeing is all about how we feel physically, psychologically, socially and emotionally. It is not just about being 'healthy' – it is about feeling good inside and out. When we talk about wellbeing, it usually encompasses the following aspects.

Physical wellbeing

- Exercising regularly to improve our physical fitness, strengthen our heart, tone our muscles, boost energy levels, elevate our mood and relieve stress through the release of endorphins – our 'feel good' hormones.
- Having good sleep habits so we can maintain focus throughout the day and be mentally alert.
- Connecting and engaging with the natural environment to reduce stress and improve our mood.
- Focusing on nutrition and a balanced diet to provide the necessary fuel our body needs.

Psychological wellbeing

- Managing our stress and anxiety while understanding and addressing any signs of depression.
- The ability to clear our minds, boost our focus and feel more at ease.
- Being open to speaking with others to help handle difficult and challenging situations, improve relationships and grow as humans.

Social wellbeing
- Establishing and maintaining positive and supportive social connections and relationships.
- Adopting communication skills to enrich these connections.

Professional wellbeing
- Balancing our personal lives with our work environment to prevent burnout.
- Creating a positive work environment to help foster work satisfaction and professional growth.

Spiritual wellbeing
- Finding meaning and purpose in life.
- Connecting with the natural world.
- Embracing and expressing gratitude.

You may have other aspects you would include – there may have even been a commercial or jingle written about them. However throughout this book, we will be focusing on these elements that contribute to the overall picture of our wellbeing.

Reflection: Rate your own wellbeing

Ask yourself the following questions to gauge your own level of wellbeing before commencing this book. You may even choose to rate yourself on the frequency at which you are able to do these things (rarely, sometimes, often).

- I handle stress, emotions and time well, and ask for help when I need it.
- I take responsibility for my actions and make careful decisions.
- I have a positive view of myself.
- I adjust well to changes and challenges while keeping balance in my life.
- I am kind to myself and do things that help me feel good and stay healthy.

- I think about what is important to me, my values and what I want in life.
- I make time to relax every day and keep balance in my life.
- I listen to others' views and get involved in causes I care about.
- I use helpful tools to take care of myself and set healthy boundaries.
- I work to create peace and balance in my relationships and community.
- I maintain a healthy diet with plenty of fruits, vegetables and water.
- I stay active by exercising regularly to keep my body strong.
- I get enough sleep each night and wake up feeling rested.
- I listen to health advice and seek help when I have concerns about my wellbeing.
- I am part of a community or interest group.
- I have a strong support network of friends and family.
- I have meaningful relationships in my life.
- I make time for my relationships and can set boundaries to prioritise my needs.
- I balance work and my personal life effectively.
- I actively learn new skills to improve my future job opportunities.
- I know the skills needed for my career interests and work on developing them.
- I am confident in my ability to work well with others and manage my time.

Wellbeing in schools

In a school context, wellbeing encompasses all of these aspects under what we would call a holistic approach – the health and happiness of students, teachers and staff. As well as physical, psychological, social, professional and spiritual wellbeing, it's common for schools to include *academic wellbeing* and *environmental wellbeing* in the mix – where opportunities for students to thrive through academic programs and the provision of safe environments for learning are also considered. This is about schools cultivating an environment that is nurturing, supporting the development of all community members and offering ways for everyone involved with the school to flourish.

For many years, schools had programs to work with students on developing their social and emotional literacy. These often included a 'one lesson a week' model and rarely crossed over into other curriculum areas. However, over the past couple of decades, there has been a significant shift in our understanding of the connection between students' social, emotional and psychological health and their academic achievement. This has created a growing evolution in how schools implement wellbeing strategies, curriculum initiatives and frameworks.

In the past, schools were primarily concerned with academic achievements and often didn't pay much attention to students' overall wellbeing. Over time, people began to recognise the importance of mental health and well-rounded human development. Educators began to see that schools were places that needed to do more than just teach subjects. They started focusing on helping students build their emotional selves and their social skills, based on the understanding that these are just as important for a student's growth as their academic success.

In the late 1990s, *positive psychology* – a term popularised by Professor Martin Seligman – emerged, providing a significant impetus to the wellbeing movement in schools. Seligman and other psychologists began moving from a deficit model of psychology to one that focused on what makes life worth living – including concepts such as happiness, wellbeing and flourishing. The field of positive psychology has grown to now encompass topics such as positive emotions, meaningful engagement, supportive relationships, resilience and character strengths.

While not all schools have openly adopted a positive psychology approach, many of the approaches being used are based on principles of positive psychology and attempt to work in the proactive rather than reactive wellbeing space.

In 2018, the Australian Government released the Australian Student Wellbeing Framework (ASWF), which was based on evidence connecting wellbeing and learning to support schools provide a strong foundation for students to reach their potential and flourish. The framework has five key pillars that are aligned to the Australian Curriculum (see figure 1 overleaf).

Some of the key practices and approaches that schools have adopted include the following:

- **Programs that target social-emotional learning (SEL)** and allow a structured approach to develop students' social and emotional skills,

with a focus on the personal and social capabilities of self-awareness and self-management along with social awareness and social management.
- **A structured wellbeing curriculum** that is scoped and sequenced according to the age of the students, and offers resources and activities around topics such as mindfulness, character strengths, respectful relationships and coping strategies.
- **An inclusive school climate** that fosters engagement, connection and support for all students to feel valued, respected and safe.

Figure 1: The Australian Student Wellbeing Framework (ASWF)

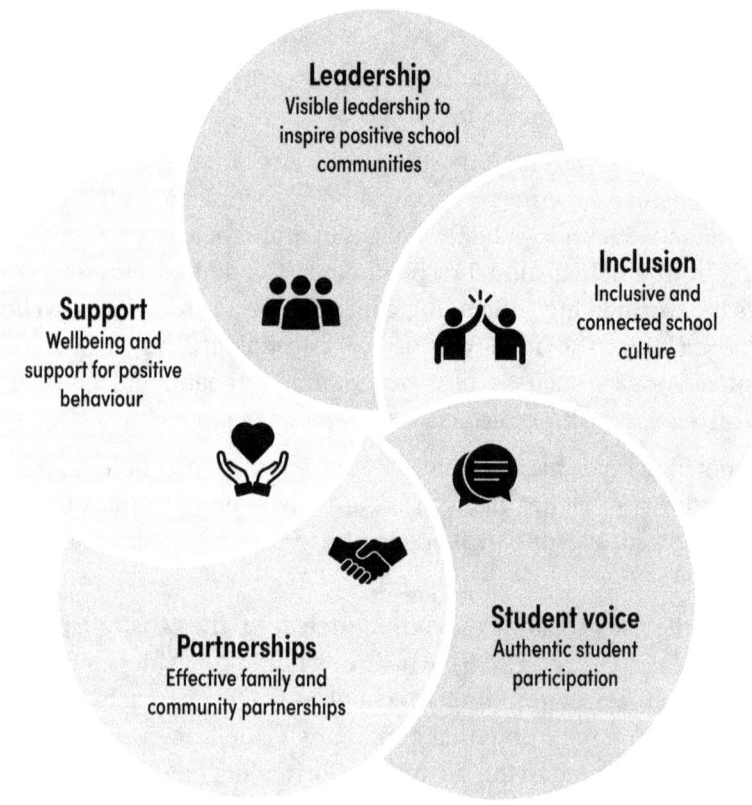

Source: © 2025 Commonwealth of Australia, https://studentwellbeinghub.edu.au.

Why teach wellbeing?

Extensive research into the impact of wellbeing initiatives in schools has shown positive outcomes, including improved academic performance, reduced behavioural problems, increased student engagement and enhanced overall wellbeing among students and staff. These findings have further encouraged schools to prioritise wellbeing as a fundamental aspect of their strategic plan, knowing that it is underpinned by a robust body of scientific research integrating findings from psychology, neuroscience and medicine.

Pioneering psychologists have found that connection, perseverance, resilience, a growth mindset and meaning contributes to human flourishing, emphasising strengths, resilience and positive emotions.

Angela Duckworth's research on grit – which she defines as perseverance and passion for long-term goals – shows that it is crucial for achieving success. Duckworth's studies have demonstrated that grit can significantly enhance students' academic performance and resilience. For instance, her research found that grit was a better predictor of academic achievement than IQ in students. Cadets at the US Military Academy who scored higher on Duckworth's Grit Scale were more likely to complete their training, despite experiencing challenges (Duckworth et al., 2007). Additionally, students with higher grit levels tended to have better grade point averages (GPAs), illustrating its impact on academic success (Duckworth et al., 2009).

Similarly, Martin Seligman's work in positive psychology underscores the benefits of wellbeing practices in schools. Seligman's research, including the Penn Resiliency Program, has shown how interventions that focus on positive emotions, such as mindfulness and gratitude, can significantly improve students' emotional health and academic performance. Participants in this program displayed increased resilience, reduced depression symptoms and better academic outcomes (Gillham et al., 2007). Seligman's broader research also indicated that positive psychology interventions, such as writing letters of gratitude, can lead to long-term increases in happiness and life satisfaction (Seligman et al., 2005). By fostering an environment that supports positive emotions and psychological strengths, schools can enhance students' overall wellbeing and academic success.

The concept of a growth mindset has also been crucial for developing wellbeing initiatives in schools. Carol Dweck's research indicates that when students adopt a growth mindset – believing that their abilities can improve with effort – they tend to show greater engagement and better academic performance. For example, in a study conducted in diverse school settings, students who were taught about the growth mindset demonstrated significant increases in motivation and achievement, particularly in challenging subjects (Dweck, 2006). This mindset also helps in reducing behavioural issues by focusing on learning from mistakes rather than fearing failure. This clearly aligns with a school's broader objectives: seeking to enhance motivation, develop a more positive attitude towards learning, overcome behavioural challenges and improve students' educational experiences. For instance, one study found that schools that implemented growth mindset interventions saw increases in student resilience and performance, as well as reductions in discipline problems (Yeager et al., 2016).

The importance of teaching coping and resilience strategies in education has also been highlighted by Professor Lea Waters' research, which emphasises the benefits of strength-based approaches for both students and teachers. Waters' studies revealed that when teachers and parents focus on students' strengths rather than weaknesses, it leads to better coping mechanisms, increased resilience, and higher engagement and motivation in their studies (Waters, 2017). For example, students who learn to identify and use their personal strengths report higher life satisfaction, and lower anxiety and depression levels (Waters, 2015). These findings demonstrate that incorporating strengths-based coping strategies into school curricula helps to enhance students' emotional and psychological wellbeing, creating a more positive and supportive learning environment

These insights highlight the importance of clearly understanding wellbeing to develop appropriate initiatives that foster supportive and effective learning environments while also building meaningful relationships. By addressing emotional, psychological and motivational aspects, schools can greatly improve outcomes for both students and staff, leading to a more positive and productive overall educational experience.

Other wellbeing resources

The topic of educator wellbeing has never been more important. Madhavi Nawana Parker and Amy Green have produced some excellent resources to help create a greater focus on self-care in an educational institution.

Educator Wellbeing by Madhavi Nawana Parker focuses on supporting educators' mental health and wellbeing. The book provides practical advice, strategies and insights to help teachers manage stress, build resilience and maintain a positive outlook. It addresses the unique challenges faced by educators and emphasises the importance of self-care and community support.

Teacher Wellbeing and *Wellbeing Leadership* by Amy Green focus on teachers' physical, emotional and mental health. They provide practical tools and strategies to help educators improve their wellbeing, cope with stress and find balance in their professional and personal lives. Both books emphasise the importance of self-care, mindfulness and developing a supportive community within the school environment.

Context is important

When looking at developing an effective wellbeing strategy, one that is impactful and relevant, it is important to have a clear understanding of your context. Our education institutions all have socioeconomic, demographic and geographic factors that create unique opportunities and challenges. Having a clear understanding of these will assist you in developing a strategic plan for wellbeing that is aligned to the school's mission and values, and those of the staff and students. Ultimately, this will lead to greater acceptance of the approach that then becomes more meaningful and relevant, and offers greater benefit to the community. This comes about as a result of being able to identify strengths and opportunities of current resources to develop strategies and initiatives that are impactful and considerate of the diverse needs of all community members.

What is wellbeing for you in your context?

Helen Street's book *Contextual Wellbeing* (2018) provides guidance around how best to define wellbeing for your setting. Street says:

> *These expressions of wellbeing and happiness recognise how we as individuals operate within and connect with our social context. Definitions of wellbeing that focus too narrowly on individual characteristics are in danger of becoming meaningless theories of everything. Wellbeing is not simply about individual expressions of thoughts, feelings and behaviours; it is not an isolated or solitary pursuit. It is just as much about the connections we form with others, the tasks we pursue and our wider sense of the world.*

To define what wellbeing means to your school and ensure it aligns with your context, consider the following (based on Street's framework):

- **Know your school culture and needs:**
    - How would you describe your school culture?
    - What impact does culture have on staff and student wellbeing?
    - Are there specific challenges or stressors that your students or staff face?
    - How do you think the different groups perceive and experience wellbeing?
- **Understand the relationships and community systems:**
    - How would you describe both the type and strength of the relationships within your school community? How might this impact wellbeing?
    - What support systems are available to promote wellbeing? How accessible are they?
- **Consider your wellbeing measures:**
    - How do you currently measure wellbeing? What indicators do you use?
    - Are there any gaps that exist in your understanding and measurement of wellbeing? How might you address them?
- **Consider how you could tailor wellbeing initiatives to your context:**
    - How are students, staff and parents involved in the development and implementation of wellbeing initiatives?
    - How are you tailoring your wellbeing initiatives to fit the unique needs and context of your school?
    - What successful practices can you include or adapt?
- **Set some goals:**
    - What short and long-term goals you can set to enhance wellbeing?
    - How can you align your goals with your school values?
    - How can you sustain and continuously improve your wellbeing initiatives?

The aim is to gain a comprehensive understanding of what wellbeing means in your specific context to help you develop effective strategies that promote a supportive and effective learning environment.

Who are school wellbeing programs for?

Wellbeing programs in schools play a crucial role in fostering a healthy and supportive educational environment, benefiting all of the stakeholders within the school environment. The initiatives and programs should all align within a framework and should be designed to enhance the overall quality of life for both staff and students by addressing their physical, emotional, social and psychological wellbeing needs.

Ultimately, if we teach wellbeing skills and concepts, our students become the primary beneficiaries. Wellbeing programs provide students with tools and resources they need to better manage their health and wellbeing, promoting a better sense of positive psychological being through resilience-building, stress reduction and support for emotional challenges they may face. By encouraging healthy lifestyles, such as regular physical activity, healthy sleep patterns and nutritious eating, these programs also help students maintain their physical health. Students also have better social-emotional learning (SEL), enhancing their interpersonal skills, sense of empathy, and both verbal and non-verbal communication, thereby creating a more supportive and inclusive school environment. Through proactive programs, students are also able to develop greater understanding of respectful relationships, make more informed choices with online safety, grow in character to resist peer pressure and have a better understanding of a culture of based on respect and inclusivity.

By teaching wellbeing concepts and skills, we provide students with a set of tools they can use to enhance their wellbeing. However, it is important to understand that not every tool will be suitable for every person or situation. Teaching students to develop their own 'bank of tools' means they will know there are different options available, allowing them to choose the appropriate tools for their individual needs and circumstances. This flexibility aims to ensure that students learn to effectively manage different challenges and maintain their own wellbeing.

As an offshoot to delivering wellbeing concepts to students, staff also benefit – both personally and professionally. Staff play a critical role in the successful implementation of wellbeing programs while role-modelling positive behaviours for students. It's only possible to do this well if staff are authentically adopting the practices in their personal lives and clearly articulating the benefits they are experiencing. To do this, professional development and ongoing support will be necessary, so staff are equipped with the skills and knowledge needed to address students' wellbeing needs and contribute to the school's overall wellbeing goals.

Embracing wellbeing practices and making wellbeing a priority in your education environment can also help strengthen the bonds between home and school. Wellbeing programs provide an opportunity for collaboration with parents and caregivers through active involvement in workshops or school-provided resources that work to reinforce the skills, concepts and practices that are taught in school. This enables families to implement similar strategies at home, thereby creating a consistent and cohesive message. Additionally, this partnership allows for a more comprehensive understanding of a student's needs, as parents and teachers share insights and observations. Ultimately, this collaborative approach ensures that students have a strong support network, promoting their wellbeing and success both in and out of the classroom, while developing the parents' knowledge of appropriate strategies and tools to try.

While school wellbeing programs are designed to benefit students, staff and families, they also address aspects that can make a positive contribution and help provide support beyond these groups and filter into the wider community. One such example is Where There's a Will – a mental health initiative in the Upper Hunter region of New South Wales, Australia, that builds on the foundation of the mental health and wellbeing programs being delivered in schools. Originating as an extension of these school-based efforts, Where There's a Will aims to expand support beyond the classroom and into the wider community. The organisation works closely with educators, students, and families with the aim of enhancing the wellbeing, mental health and resilience strategies that are being taught in schools. The initiative offers additional resources, workshops and community events to ensure that young people and their families have the tools and knowledge to manage mental health challenges. Through this comprehensive approach, Where There's a Will seeks to create a cohesive support network throughout the Upper Hunter (South Australia), promoting a culture of understanding and proactive mental health care. This demonstrates the power of connection between schools and the wider community.

Wellbeing does not mean happiness

While fleeting happiness, joy and pleasure are often mistaken for true fulfillment, it is the deeper, more stable elements such as purpose and meaningful relationships that define genuine wellbeing and can transform our approach to mental health. So why are happiness and wellbeing often discussed together as a singular concept?

Happiness refers to a subjective state of mind that can be characterised by our sense that 'life is good' or as a result of feelings of joy, excitement and pleasure. But it is a temporary state that is influenced by immediate experiences and thoughts. Wellbeing may encompass periods of happiness but it also includes elements such as meaningful relationships, a sense of purpose, accomplishments and physical health, making it a more enduring and comprehensive state of being.

Any wellbeing initiative should provide clarity and opportunity for understanding that wellbeing does not solely rely on happiness. Part of any successful wellbeing strategy is to develop mechanisms to accept and deal with situations where our engagement, connections or sense of purpose is being challenged.

Understanding the differences between hedonic and eudaimonic wellbeing helps broaden our awareness. *Hedonic wellbeing* focuses on looking for happiness, finding pleasure and deliberately avoiding discomfort. We then bask in these moments, enjoying happiness and satisfaction right away, rather than thinking about long-term fulfillment. Whereas *eudaimonic wellbeing* involves working towards finding meaning and purpose in our lives. It focuses on personal growth, fulfilling our potential and doing things that make us feel fulfilled and truly satisfied in the long run.

Clearly, learning to deal with the ups and downs of life, understanding that bad times are temporary and that it is okay to not consistently feel happiness can enhance both eudaimonic and hedonic wellbeing. This fosters resilience and growth, and helps individuals find meaning and purpose in their challenges (eudaimonic). It helps people manage their emotions and supports overall happiness (hedonic).

Reflection: Happiness and wellbeing

Reflection 1
- Give yourself permission to feel any emotion (pleasant, unpleasant or neutral).
- Greet your feelings with kind attention, like a loving parent comforting a child.

Reflection 2
- List some things that make you happy.
- List some times when you have felt deep wellbeing.
- Compare the lists and note similarities and differences.
- Reflect on what helps you cultivate wellbeing.

Reflection 3
- Think of wellbeing as a deep well of nourishment.
- Identify what nourishes you in life.
- Reflect on whether these things have changed over time.

Reflection 4
- Identify a place where you experience wellbeing (in nature or in your imagination).
- Describe how wellbeing feels in your mind and body in this place. Compare this feeling to times when you have felt happy.
- Reflect on how your mind and imagination can help you experience wellbeing.
- Identify mental states (such as perspective, mindful awareness) and bodily states (such as calm, peaceful, relaxed) that help you cultivate your wellbeing.

The importance of resilience for staff

The landscape of education is ever-evolving. Educators are key to sustaining learning environments that shape the minds of future generations. However, it is no secret that working in an educational institution comes with a unique set of challenges that may sometimes feel overwhelming. From managing students with diverse learning and emotional needs to navigating the ever-increasing administrative demands, it is no wonder educators are reporting increased feelings of pressure and decreased ability to cope with expectations. There is a clear need to work at developing resilience in educators for both their professional effectiveness and their personal wellbeing.

When asked, teachers I speak with report the following as significant challenges that they face.

Top three professional challenges:

1. **High workload:** Teachers often manage large classes, extensive lesson planning, assessments, individual learning plans and co-curricular activities.
2. **Emotional demands:** Dealing with students' personal issues, behavioural problems and diverse learning needs resulting in significant demands on emotional energy.
3. **Administrative pressures:** Teachers report that the documentation required around social, emotional, behavioural and learning needs can become challenging depending on the number of students and incidents being dealt with. In addition, following up attendance, doubling up on reporting processes (continuous and end of semester) and responding to emails creates additional demands on their time.

Top three personal challenges:

1. **Work-life balance:** Balancing professional responsibilities with personal life can be difficult.
2. **Mental health:** The cumulative stress from the various demands and responsibilities can impact teachers' mental health, causing anxiety, depression and burnout.
3. **Social pressures:** Societal expectations and scrutiny of teachers' performance can add to their stress. Judgements on their level of professionalism have an impact.

Developing resilience to cope with these is very important.

What is resilience?

Defining resilience can be challenging. Many people have their own definition that works to suit their context. When you are defining what you think resilience might be, are you considering the range of perspectives – psychological, physical, emotional and economic, or even a general understanding of what resilience in education may be? Are you including behaviours you expect to see from your staff and/or students?

I believe that resilience can be defined as:

The ability to bounce back from adversity, adapt to challenging situations, and thrive even when facing difficult circumstances.

When we transfer this to our experience as educators, resilience may mean the ability to maintain our passion and enthusiasm for teaching and to stay hopeful despite any obstacles that come our way. It doesn't mean that we don't acknowledge the challenges, but rather we are capable of continuing to motivate and support our students despite the difficulties we're facing. It is an understanding that we can develop and build on our resilience helping us take calculated risks, capitalise on opportunities and achieve success. As educators, our ability to bounce back from adversity is not fixed. Like any skill, it can be developed.

Therefore, the key understandings of resilience include:

- Resilient people **bounce** rather than **breaking** when faced with an adversity or challenge.
- Resilience **can be developed**. Everyone can enhance their resilience by developing resilience competencies.

If resilience is a dynamic and developable skill rather than a fixed trait, that means it is something we can build on over time. It is about being flexible in how we think and approach challenges; being able to change our perspective and adapt when things don't go as planned; being able to stay calm and regulate our emotions; and practising self-care. Remember, we may not be able to control or change a situation, but we are able to control how we feel and how we respond.

The ability to adapt to challenging situations does not apply only to monumental events; simple daily activities can test and strengthen our resilience. Each day we face situations that can be opportunities to develop our ability to cope. For example: plans changing, having a sick child, giving a presentation at work, starting a new job or having our car break down – all of these are opportunities to build resilience. These routine challenges teach us to remain flexible, maintain a positive attitude and develop problem-solving skills. By approaching daily difficulties with resilience, we not only learn to handle stress more effectively but also grow more confident in our ability to cope with larger challenges in the future.

It is also important to challenge the myths that exist about resilience. Take a look at table 1.

Table 1: Resilience myths and facts

Myth	Fact
Resilient people have 'tough skin' and do not show emotions.	Resilient people are able to regulate their emotions.
Resilient people are able to do it all on their own.	Resilient people ask for help as part of their resilience strategies.
Resilience is something you either have or you don't.	Resilience can be developed over time.
Resilient people don't experience stress or challenging times.	Resilient people manage stress and challenges with effective coping strategies.
Resilient people accept everything, even if it seems unfair.	Resilient people problem-solve by finding ways to address issues.
Resilient people always act fast and can make quick decisions.	Resilient people know when to slow down.

Resilience in a school context

Resilience is essential for people working within an educational context.

Resilient staff are more effective in managing their learning environments. They are able to maintain a sense of calm and create positive learning environments, even when behavioural issues are occurring. This, in turn, enhances student engagement and learning outcomes, builds stronger relationships and provides essential encouragement and support.

The ever-changing landscape of education can be challenging if staff are not adaptable and agile in their approach. Resilient educators demonstrate the ability to navigate the many complexities, such as changes in curriculum, technological advancement, and new educational policies and practices, without becoming distressed or letting these changes affect their ability to stay positive and effective in the profession.

When staff are able to navigate the ups and downs of their career with resilience, this can assist them to remain in the education profession.

They will be better equipped to manage stress and prevent burnout, maintain a positive outlook and cope with the emotional demands of their job. Ultimately, this will lead to better mental health and more fulfilling personal and professional lives.

Furthermore, resilience encourages personal growth by enabling educators to learn from their experiences and challenges, fostering a mindset of continuous improvement and self-reflection, which is crucial for personal development.

Developing resilience

Karen Reivich and Andrew Shatté's *The Resilience Factor: 7 Essential Skills for Overcoming Life's Inevitable Obstacles* (2003) offers practical guidance on how we can develop resilience. The book outlines seven key skills that can help individuals build resilience and better manage challenges in their personal and professional lives:

1. **Regulating emotions:** Accurately identifying and naming emotions, using mindfulness to stay present and aware, and employing cognitive restructuring to shift negative thought patterns to more balanced ones.
2. **Controlling impulses:** Managing impulsive reactions, recognising triggers, using 'pause-and-plan' techniques such as counting to ten or deep breathing, and developing problem-solving strategies to help us handle challenging situations.
3. **Enhancing optimism:** Cultivating a balanced mindset, recognising when we focus on negative thoughts, understanding how to practise realistic optimism by balancing positive thinking with realistic assessments, and encouraging supportive self-talk.
4. **Cultivating cognitive clarity:** Avoiding cognitive distortions such as personalising or catastrophising our thinking, making accurate attributions to avoid unfair blame, and seeing setbacks as learning opportunities.
5. **Developing a greater sense of empathy:** Learning to fully engage in active listening to understand others' perspectives. Learning to interpret the non-verbal cues, and validate others' feelings respectfully, even if we disagree.
6. **Building self-efficacy:** Setting achievable goals by breaking them into smaller steps, focusing on developing our own strengths, and cultivating persistence to help us overcome challenges.

7. **Creating connections**: Building and maintaining supportive relationships, taking calculated risks to help us grow, and knowing how to seek help when needed.

There are several specific approaches that can help develop resilience in educators. These include:

- **Developing cognitive clarity:**
  - Ongoing professional development is crucial, focusing on areas such as stress management, classroom management and emotional intelligence to equip educators with the necessary skills to navigate challenges effectively.

- **Creating connections:**
  - Mentorship programs and support networks within schools can provide educators with a sense of community and the opportunity to share experiences, reducing feelings of isolation.
  - Creating a positive and supportive work environment, where educators' efforts are recognised and a culture of respect and appreciation is fostered, further enhances resilience.

- **Encouraging emotional regulation:**
  - Encouraging educators to engage in reflective practices, such as journalling or peer discussions, helps them process experiences, gain insights and develop a growth mindset, contributing to continuous learning and resilience.

- **Building self-efficacy:**
  - Making goal-setting a regular practice with achievable endpoints helps to build self-efficacy which contributes to resilience. Prioritise celebrating the success of goal achievement to reward and encourage further goals to be set.

- **Prioritising self-care:**
  - Encouraging self-care practices, such as regular exercise, meditation, and engaging in hobbies, supports educators' physical and mental wellbeing. Schools can facilitate this by promoting a healthy work-life balance and providing resources for self-care.

Activities: Building resilience

- Develop a resilience map – a visual timeline of your professional journey – marking significant challenges and how you overcame them.
- Keep a journal to reflect on your daily experiences, including challenges and ways in which you overcame them.
- Create a personal resilience action plan, in which you identify specific goals and strategies to enhance your resilience in both your professional and personal life.
- Set yourself a resilience challenge: design a small, manageable challenge that pushes you out of your comfort zone. Find a way to frame the challenge as a positive opportunity for you to practise and develop your resilience skills.
- Brainstorm:
  - The strengths, skills and abilities you believe to be crucial for developing your resilience. Rank yourself on a scale of 1–5 based on where you feel you sit for each of them.
  - Your own list of myths and facts about what resilience is or isn't.

CHAPTER 2
SPEAKING THE LANGUAGE OF WELLBEING
The Foundation for Flourishing

Speak a shared language of wellbeing, define your terms, cultivate emotional literacy and harness your character strengths to thrive together.

Building a shared language of wellbeing in any institution is essential if we want to create a unified and consistent approach to supporting staff and students. When we all speak the same language and use the same terminology, this helps reduce misunderstandings while ensuring better opportunities for clear communication, consistent practices and a unified ethos. This consistency helps us implement wellbeing initiatives, enhance support for staff and students and foster a positive school culture through common understanding. In addition, a common language helps align the school's vision and values, making it easier for all school members to collaborate, adopt and apply wellbeing principles in their daily lives.

Having a common language of wellbeing allows for better measurement and evaluation of initiatives, thereby helping schools make data-driven improvements. As schools grow or new staff members join, having a shared language ensures smooth integration of new practices and maintains the school's commitment to a supportive and healthy environment for everyone. Being consistent with language also helps avoid any misrepresentation to the parent community by ensuring clear communication and creating a cohesive support system for students.

If our ultimate goal is to create an environment that helps community members move towards a happier and more fulfilling life, concepts such as wellbeing, positive education, positive psychology, gratitude, resilience, empathy, character strengths and mindfulness all play a critical role. We understand that these skills and ideas form the basis of how we can improve our lives and the lives of others. Therefore, within our own context, we must establish a clear, consistent and shared definition and understanding of the terms and language we use.

Defining wellbeing in your context

Establishing a definition of wellbeing in a school context involves considering the school community's unique needs and goals. As discussed earlier, Helen Street's Contextual Wellbeing Framework provides a clear path to include the people, space, policies and social norms as you work to construct your definition of wellbeing that aligns to your site.

Here's an example of an approach to define wellbeing in your context:

1. **Engage members of your school community:**
   - **Staff:** teachers, administrators and support staff – it is important to understand everyone's perspectives on what wellbeing means for them in the school environment.
   - **Students:** learn about the students' wellbeing needs and their priorities through focus groups or use of an Appreciative Inquiry (we'll explore this concept in chapter 5).
   - **Community:** bring community members into the conversation to gather a holistic view of wellbeing.

2. **Review existing frameworks:**
   - **Current models within the school:** what wellbeing frameworks are currently established within the school environment?
   - **Best practices:** review established wellbeing frameworks such as the PERMA model (positive emotion, engagement, relationships, meaning, achievement), the Five Ways to Wellbeing and Visible Wellbeing.

3. **Define the key components you want to include; for example:**
   - **Environmental:** safe, inclusive and supportive, natural and classroom.
   - **Emotional:** resilience, self-esteem, positive emotions, coping, emotional regulation and psychological support.
   - **Physical:** nutrition, exercise and sleep.
   - **Social:** values, relationships, social skills and belonging.
   - **Academic:** achievement and engagement.

4. **Draft a definition:**
   - Combine the information into a single definition. For example, 'Wellbeing is a holistic state of emotional, social and physical health, supported by an environment that promotes positive relationships, engagement, growth and resilience.'

5. **Seek feedback:**
   - Share the draft definition with the community for feedback.

6. **Communicate the final definition:**
   - Once finalised, communicate the definition clearly to the school community.

7. **Update policies:**
   - Ensure policies and procedures reflect ways to deliver the definition you have established.

Understanding commonly used terms

The world of wellbeing in a school environment has a number of terms that are used in various situations. After you have established a clear definition of wellbeing, it is important for staff to also have a shared understanding of other commonly used terms. Let's take a look at some of them.

Positive psychology is the study of what makes life enjoyable and fulfilling.

Martin Seligman and Mihaly Csikszentmihalyi (2000) define positive psychology as 'The scientific study of positive human functioning and flourishing on multiple levels that include the biological, personal, relational, institutional, cultural, and global dimensions of life'.

Instead of just focusing on treating problems, positive psychology emphasises enhancing positive experiences, traits and institutions. Understanding positive psychology can help us find more meaning in life, build stronger relationships and improve overall wellbeing. Research by psychologists such as Barbara Fredrickson, who developed the broaden-and-build theory, supports the importance of positive emotions in promoting psychological resilience and building relationships. Fredrickson (2009) writes, 'Positive emotions broaden your sense of possibility and open your mind, allowing you to build new skills and resources that provide value in other areas of life'.

Positive education combines academic learning with the ideas from positive psychology. In addition to traditional academics this approach focuses on teaching students skills such as resilience, happiness and character development.

Positive education is an umbrella term used to describe empirically validated interventions and programs from positive psychology that have an impact on student wellbeing (White & Murray, 2015).

Strengths can refer to talents which must be clearly identified as different to character strengths. Talents are natural abilities, such as being good at a specific sport, playing an instrument or solving complex problems.

Character strengths, on the other hand, are positive traits such as kindness, perseverance and creativity that are part of who we are as individuals.

By recognising and leveraging our talents and character strengths, we can become more engaged and satisfied with our lives. Understanding the difference between talents and character strengths allows us to work towards our goals more effectively and contribute positively to our communities. This distinction is explored in the work of researchers such as Christopher Peterson and Martin Seligman, who developed the VIA (values in action) classification of character strengths, which we explore later in this chapter.

Gratitude is the act of being thankful and appreciating the good things in life. Practising gratitude has been shown to improve mental health, relationships and overall wellbeing. When we all understand the value of gratitude, this can create a culture of positivity and support in our communities. The benefits of gratitude have been extensively researched by psychologists such as Robert Emmons who has demonstrated its positive impact on mental health and wellbeing. Emmons (2007) writes, 'Gratitude is a recognition of goodness, that we are receiving something of value. It enables us to connect to something greater than ourselves.'

Resilience is the ability to bounce back from challenges and setbacks. It is about being able to handle difficult situations and adapt to change. Understanding resilience can help us develop coping strategies and a mindset that helps us grow stronger through adversity. The American Psychological Association (APA) has published several resources and research papers on the importance of resilience in maintaining mental health and coping with stress. The APA (2019) states, 'Resilience is the process and outcome of successfully adapting to difficult or challenging life experiences, especially through mental, emotional and behavioural flexibility and adjustment to external and internal demands.'

Empathy is the ability to understand and share the feelings of others. It is crucial for building meaningful relationships and fostering a compassionate society. When we all understand empathy, we can communicate better, support each other and create a more caring community. Researchers such as Daniel Batson have extensively studied empathy and its role in promoting prosocial behaviour. Batson (2011) explains, 'Empathy-induced altruism leads to helping others, even at a cost to oneself.'

Mindfulness is about being present in the moment and paying attention to what is happening around us without judgement. It helps us become more aware of our thoughts and feelings and can reduce stress and improve emotional regulation. By understanding mindfulness, we can live more intentionally and improve our overall wellbeing.

Hugh van Cuylenburg, founder of the Resilience Project, is one of the great proponents of mindfulness. He advocates for the benefits of mindfulness on emotional health and wellbeing, stating, 'Mindfulness can lead to a reduction in anxiety and stress, as well as an increase in focus and attention, all of which contribute to a more resilient and fulfilled life' (van Cuylenburg, 2020).

Developing a shared understanding of these important wellbeing terms is crucial for personal growth and creating supportive communities. When all staff use the same definitions, students can develop a clear, consistent understanding of these concepts and how to apply them to their lives. This consistency promotes happiness, resilience and wellbeing for everyone.

Emotional literacy

With the increased understanding of how wellbeing impacts learning, education has evolved to deliver a more well-rounded experience. As a result, emotional literacy has become a key aspect of teaching. Emotional literacy means being able to recognise, understand and manage our own emotions, as well as empathise with others' emotions. This skill helps students have positive social interactions and build healthy relationships both in and outside of school.

Emotional literacy is important because it can help students do better in school, communicate more effectively, make better decisions and become more emotionally resilient. Emotionally literate students can manage stress better, face challenges with confidence, and engage well with their peers and teachers.

To integrate emotional literacy into the curriculum, teachers can use activities that boost self-awareness and empathy, such as group discussions, role-playing and reflection exercises. Emotional literacy principles can also be included in existing subjects for a more complete learning experience. It is also important to train and support teachers in teaching emotional literacy effectively.

Emotional literacy is a complex skill that includes several key elements:

- **Self-awareness:** Recognising our emotions and their impact on thoughts and behaviours.

- **Self-regulation:** Managing emotions effectively and adapting to changing circumstances.
- **Social awareness:** Understanding and empathising with others' emotions and experiences.
- **Relationship skills:** Building and maintaining healthy, supportive relationships.
- **Decision-making:** Making thoughtful choices based on ethical considerations and understanding consequences.

By learning these skills, students can better manage their emotions and interactions, leading to improved success in school and their life beyond. Examples may be through:

- **Academic success:** Emotionally literate students are better equipped to manage stress and anxiety, which can improve focus and concentration. This, in turn, can lead to better academic performance.
- **Improved relationships:** Students who understand and regulate their emotions can communicate more effectively and build stronger, healthier relationships with their peers, teachers and family members.
- **Deeper levels of empathy:** Emotional literacy promotes empathy, allowing students to understand and appreciate a wider range of perspectives. This can lead to more inclusive and supportive learning environments.
- **Increased levels of resilience:** Emotionally literate students are better able to cope with challenges and setbacks, making them more resilient in the face of adversity.
- **Psychological wellbeing:** By learning to manage their emotions, students can reduce the risk of developing anxiety and depression.
- **Increased levels of judgement:** Students with strong emotional literacy are more likely to make thoughtful ethical choices in various situations.

Examples: How to integrate emotional literacy into the classroom

- **Teach mindfulness:** Teaching students mindfulness techniques, such as breathing exercises and being in and savouring the moment, can help them become more aware of their emotions and develop

self-regulation skills. It can also increase compassion for self and others and increase our ability to remain attentive.
- **Choose a social-emotional learning (SEL) program:** This will help students understand degrees of emotion, pay attention to their and others' emotions and become more aware of appropriate responses – in turn, building stronger relationships.
- **Incorporate sharing circles or circle time:** Creating a safe and open environment where students can discuss their feelings and experiences can promote emotional awareness and empathy.
- **Explore curriculum:** Introducing students to curriculum that explores emotional experiences, such as literature and art, can provide opportunities for reflection and discussion about emotions and relationships.

Example: An emotional literacy program

'Kimochi' is the Japanese word for 'feelings'. The Kimochi program consists of plush toys designed to help children express themselves as they learn about feeling-driven behaviours. Children explore how to manage feelings such as being mad, sad, happy, frustrated, left out or brave. They engage in activities focused on building emotional intelligence, self-esteem and resilience, and understanding degrees of emotion. Each emotion is explored through a process of connection, communication, creation and practice

Kimochi helps students develop the skills to understand their feelings, to communicate their feelings to others and to develop positive relationships, while managing conflict and challenges.

Character strengths

> *Watch your thoughts, for they become your words.*
> *Watch your words, for they become your actions.*
> *Watch your actions, for they become your habits.*
> *Watch your habits, for they become your character.*
> *Watch your character, for it becomes your destiny.*

– Lao Tzu

Lao Tzu's famous quote connects character with who we want to be. In positive psychology terms, we acknowledge our character through character strengths. We use this understanding to lift ourselves when we're feeling low and to recognise our best selves when things are going well.

Using the language of character strengths as part of a whole-school approach to wellbeing allows us to effectively integrate the principles of positive psychology into everyday interactions across the school, based on a shared vocabulary.

Most of the time we think character strengths are things that we're good at, and this isn't wrong. However, from a psychological point of view, the key components that constitute a character strength are that:

- They are a positive quality or attribute
- They energise us
- When we choose to use them, we perform well at them.

The VIA character strengths were developed by over 50 psychologists, led by Christopher Petersen and Martin Seligman over a three-year period. The aim was to identify universal character strengths that cross culture, race, religion, gender or education. They might look different in different cultures but nevertheless these universal strengths still exist.

There are 24 character strengths which are grouped into six virtues: wisdom, courage, humanity, justice, temperance and transcendence.

Ultimately, character strengths help us further understand our identity through knowing who we are when we are our best self. Niemiec and McGrath (2019) state:

> *Character strengths are basic elements of our identity. When we express these character strengths through our thoughts and actions, research, says, we tend to feel happier, more connected, and more productive.*

It is important to remember that there is a difference between talents, skills and character strengths. Talents are things that we are good at (perhaps a natural ability), for example the ability to play music. Skills are things we can develop, such as public speaking or completing a Rubik's cube. Some of these may form a passion or interest, but they are not directly linked to how we see ourselves. Character strengths are a scientifically validated classification of positive traits in human beings. These strengths are the core capacities for thinking, feeling and behaving in ways that are beneficial both to ourselves and those around us. They represent the qualities that are universally valued across cultures, and that contribute to wellbeing.

Importantly, when we remember that character strengths focus on 'what is right with us', we move towards establishing a school culture that builds on the strengths of who our staff and students are. Focusing on character strengths can enhance wellbeing in several ways; let's look at some of these.

Self-awareness and personal growth

The character strengths framework helps staff and students identify their unique strengths. This self-awareness gives everyone a more positive understanding of self and of areas of lesser strength, enhancing overall personal growth.

Positive relationships

When we recognise and appreciate each other's character strengths, we build understanding, empathy, respect and trust within the school community. This strengthens interpersonal relationships and promotes a supportive environment where everyone feels valued and understood.

Furthermore, when character strengths are interwoven with the school culture, we promote inclusivity and appreciation for all. Students are encouraged to recognise and celebrate the unique strengths of their peers, ultimately fostering a sense of belonging and connection.

Resilience

Students learn to apply their character strengths to cope with various challenges they face, to manage levels of anxiety and to maintain a positive mindset, ultimately enhancing their ability to navigate through life's ups and downs.

Character strengths align closely with many social-emotional learning (SEL) frameworks to help develop self-awareness, social awareness and responsible decision-making. Incorporating strengths-based practices into SEL programs equips students with essential skills for managing emotions, building positive relationships and making constructive choices which can lead to improved resilience.

Engagement and accomplishment

When students have an appreciation of their character strengths in action, and teachers tailor teaching strategies to incorporate these into their approaches, students are more motivated and engaged in their school experiences.

In essence, using the VIA character strengths in a school environment enhances self-awareness, strengthens relationships, fosters resilience, supports academic engagement, prepares students for future success and creates a positive and inclusive school culture. These benefits collectively contribute to a holistic approach to education that nurtures the whole child and prepares them for a fulfilling and successful life.

Things to keep in mind when using character strengths

- Focus on the language of strengths and lesser strengths rather than using the term 'weaknesses'.
- No one should have to change from 'their best self' when they enter the school grounds. How do we embrace each student's individuality within our environment?

Some questions to ask:

- What is right with you?
- When do you feel the most 'you'?
- How could a focus on character strengths make your teaching more effective?
- What are some of your strengths that you want to make sure are included in your teaching?
- How can you ensure that you are bringing your character strengths to your role in your school?
- How can you identify and nurture the character strengths of the students in your care?

Identifying and using character strengths

The 24 VIA character strengths, categorised into six virtues, are listed in table 2 overleaf.

Table 2: The VIA classification of 24 character strengths

Wisdom	**Creativity** Clever Original and Adaptive Problem-solver	**Curiosity** Interested Explores new things Open to new ideas	**Judgement** Critical thinker Thinks things through Open-minded	**Love of learning** Masters new skills and topics Systematically adds to knowledge	**Perspective** Wise Provides wise counsel Takes the big-picture view
Courage	**Bravery** Shows valour Doesn't shrink from fear Speaks up for what's right	**Perseverance** Persistent Industrious Finishes what one starts	**Honesty** Authentic Trustworthy Sincere	**Zest** Enthusiastic Energetic Doesn't do things half-heartedly	
Humanity	**Love** Warm and genuine Values close relationships	**Kindness** Generous Nurturing Caring Compassionate Altruistic	**Social intelligence** Areare of the motives and feelings of self/others Knows what makes others tick		

Justice	**Teamwork** Team player Socially responsible Loyal	**Fairness** Just Doesn't let feelings bias decisions about others	**Leadership** Organises group activities Encourages a group to get things done		
Temperance	**Forgiveness** Merciful Accepts others' shortcomings Gives people a second chance	**Humility** Modest Lets one's accomplishments speak for themselves	**Prudence** Careful Cautious Doesn't take undue risks	**Self-regulation** Self-controlled Disciplined Manages impulses and emotions	
Transcendence	**Appreciation of beauty and excellence** Feels awe and wonder in beauty Inspired by goodness of others	**Gratitude** Thankful for the good Expresses thanks Feels blessed	**Hope** Optimistic Future-minded Future-orientated	**Humour** Playful Brings smiles to others Lighthearted	**Spirituality** Searches for meaning Feels a sense of purpose Senses a relationship with the sacred

Source: © 2004–2025, VIA Institute on Character. All rights reserved. Used with permission. www.viacharacter.org.

The VIA Institute of Character website, viacharacter.org, provides amazing resources that help people:

- Discover and understand their strengths
- Learn ways to boost their strengths
- Find ways to build strengths into their lives.

It is important to find the right balance when using character strengths. To do this, we must understand that character strengths also have a 'shadow side' – where there is an unintended negative effect from a strength being overused.

Finding the right balance is referred to as the Golden Mean, where we use the right 'amount' of our character strengths in the right way. For example, in a school context, someone who has *humour and playfulness* as their top strength must learn about when, where and how it is appropriate to engage with this strength. Overplaying this strength can have a negative impact on themselves, the people around them and the learning environment.

Activity: The Golden Mean

Draw a balanced see-saw for a character strength. On one side write some words to describe what it might look like if the strength was *underused*. On the other side, write some words to describe what it might look like if the strength was *overused*. In the middle, write words that describe how the optimal use of the strength may present.

For example:

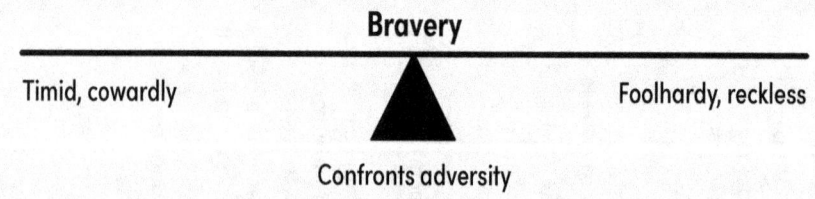

Once you have drawn these, refer to them and monitor your behaviour, helping you develop greater awareness to balance your strengths and use them appropriately in your daily life.

It is critical to stress the importance of having a common understanding and definition for each of the character strengths. It is not helpful for anyone if the meaning of each strength changes depending on who is engaging in the discussion. For example, a consistent approach to what it means to be brave, whether in the science lab, on the sports field or on the theatre stage, provides a clear understanding of what it looks like, how it feels and what can be done to nurture, develop or balance this trait.

For students to clearly understand all 24 character strengths, it is important that a staggered, sequential approach that is aligned to your curriculum framework is implemented.

During my time at St Peter's College, Adelaide, we developed the plan featured in table 3 after we determined that the randomised teaching of character strengths was not gaining the depth of understanding that we hoped.

Table 3: The character strengths of a flourishing life

Year	Constant	Strength 1	Strength 2	Strength 3	Strength 4	
Rec	Gratitude	Honesty	Perseverance	Kindness	Fairness	
1	Gratitude	Curiosity	Forgiveness	Love	Humour	Plus revisit previous 4
2	Gratitude	Creativity	Zest	Appreciation of beauty	Gratitude	Plus revisit previous 8
3	Gratitude	Love of learning	Self regulation	Bravery	Hope	Plus revisit previous 12
4	Gratitude	Judgement	Prudence	Spirituality	Teamwork	Plus revisit previous 16
5	Gratitude	Perspective	Humility	Social intelligence	Leadership	Plus revisit previous 20
6	Gratitude	Understanding of all 24 strengths				

Wisdom	Courage	Humanity	Justice	Temperance	Transcendence

Source: St Peter's College, 2019.

The aim of this was to assign four character strengths that would be taught explicitly throughout the assigned year. This didn't mean that the other strengths were not explored, but rather they may not have been covered in as much detail. You will notice that 'gratitude' was a 'constant' strength covered each year. This was a deliberate choice, based on the belief that gratitude fosters kindness and love.

Character strengths in action

One of the most significant benefits of incorporating character strengths into your school is that they do not need to become an 'add on'; often, they simply require some tweaks to current practice and pedagogy. This means that you don't need to change what you have been teaching. An example of shifting the language can be seen in table 4.

Table 4: Examples of incorporating character strengths into current practice

Subject	Current activity	Activity incorporating character strengths
Humanities and Social Sciences (HASS)	Researching historical leaders.	Include questions about character strengths: • What made this person a great leader? • What character strengths did this person have and how did they display them? • What could you learn from this person? • Is there a time when you feel these strengths could work against the leader?
HASS	Creating a family tree.	Students include the character strengths of their family members.
English or pastoral care	Writing a narrative about their identity.	Have students include who they are 'at their best' including their character strengths. Collate these into a class book so all students can learn about each other.

Subject	Current activity	Activity incorporating character strengths
English	Creative writing.	Rewrite the ending of a known story by shifting the focus of the character strength. For example, what would have happened if Pinocchio didn't use his strength of honesty?
English	Literature review.	Instead of only focusing on the physical and emotional characteristics of characters in a novel study, include their character strengths. In younger years, students can explore this by: • Naming a character • Naming a strength they used • Identifying the evidence to show they used their strength through something they DID and something they SAID.
Physical Education	Learning new skills.	Incorporate character strength language to include words such as 'perseverance', 'bravery', 'zest' and 'creativity'.
Visual Art	Self-representation project.	Students list their strengths in a word cloud format to graphically represent them as part of their identity.
Music	Creating your soundtrack.	Students create a playlist of songs that reflect their character strengths.

Character strengths are not fixed

Character strengths are not fixed, and can evolve over time and in different situations. Research in personality over the past decade has shown us that our character strengths are flexible and can be developed. This means that while your top strengths may stay consistent for a period, they can shift and adapt to meet the demands of your life. Understanding that strengths are changeable allows us to actively cultivate and enhance them. By recognising and embracing the potential for growth, we learn to see and develop our strengths as dynamic and adaptable qualities, leading to personal growth and resilience.

There are ways we can work to develop our character strengths: personally, if we want to grow our own, or by teaching them within our classroom context, if we want to help others grow their strengths.

Here are some ways to develop strengths:

- In your next conversation, listen carefully before sharing your ideas (perspective).
- Avoid bragging about your achievements for a week and see how your relationships improve (humility).
- Take a moment to picture a future where you are your best self and everything is going well.
- Make sure this vision is realistic and positive. Then, think about the strengths you need to make it happen (hope).
- Put yourself in the shoes of someone who you may have wronged and try to understand their perspective (forgiveness).

Online character strengths resources

At My Best	Positive psychology tools for adults' professional growth	atmybest.com
GoStrengths!	Character strength development Emotional intelligence Resilience Goal-setting	gostrengths.com
Let it Ripple	*The Science of Character* film Character Strength Day	letitripple.org/ scienceofcharacter
Strength Clusters	Making strengths real, visible and tangible	strengthclusters.com
VIA	24 character strengths	viacharacter.org

CHAPTER 3
INSPIRING TRUST AND GROWTH
It All Starts with Staff

Be your best self to inspire others, build connections that strengthen trust and foster a feedback culture that empowers growth.

There are a lot of inspirational quotes I could include in this section: 'Happy employees do a better job and create happier customers'; 'Improving employee happiness improves productivity'... Whichever quote you choose to connect with, the truth will always be that taking care of your staff is fundamental to the success of any educational institution or organisation. When employees feel valued and supported, they are more likely to be engaged, motivated, creative and productive. Institutions that invest in staff wellbeing will create a positive work environment where individuals have the means to thrive, have high morale and ultimately remain engaged with the organisation. Happy and healthy staff have higher levels of engagement and are more resilient and better equipped to handle challenges, leading to improved performance and overall success.

Building staff capacity through professional development is crucial to help employees develop and enrich their craft, growing in their knowledge, skills and roles. Investing in staff development not only benefits the individuals but also the institution, as it leads to a staff more aligned to the organisation's vision and mission. When employees see that their employers are committed to their growth, they are more likely to feel a sense of loyalty, respect and dedication to the institution.

Strong relationships and a sense of connection based on trust and respect are crucial for fostering a collaborative and cohesive environment. When staff feel connected to their colleagues and leaders, they are more likely to communicate openly, share ideas and work collaboratively. Strong bonds of trust contribute to a supportive environment where employees feel comfortable taking risks and voicing their opinions, ultimately leading to better problem-solving and increased creativity. In essence, looking after your staff, building their capacity and fostering connections are essential components for a thriving and successful institution.

When you're wanting to introduce wellbeing practices, policies and curriculum into your environment, it is vital that staff are educated in the skills, concepts and practices before delivering them to students. Staff who are trained and are embracing these wellbeing strategies and techniques in their own lives can teach others from a place of personal experience and understanding, making their instruction more credible and relatable. There is a greater level of authenticity when sharing their benefits. Additionally, staff serve as role models for students by embodying wellbeing practices, setting a positive example that students are more likely to follow. This helps create a supportive environment where students receive guidance and reinforcement through the provision of clear and consistent messaging through a school-wide approach to wellbeing. Furthermore, staff who are trained in wellbeing practices are better equipped to understand the potential challenges students may face in adopting these practices. This empathy allows them to offer better support and adapt their teaching strategies to meet students' needs.

On a personal level, these wellbeing practices can also enhance staff members' own mental and emotional health, leading to increased levels of resilience while lowering levels of anxiety and depression. This will, ultimately, help staff feel a greater sense of satisfaction and overall effectiveness in their personal and professional roles. By understanding and implementing these practices themselves, staff can look after their own wellbeing, enabling them to better support their students.

Finally, when staff are knowledgeable about wellbeing they can create a more supportive and understanding environment through their use of language. This helps in identifying students who might need additional support and providing timely interventions.

Overall, developing and equipping school staff in wellbeing practices and the language of wellbeing equips them with the knowledge and skills to effectively teach and support students, fostering a healthier and more positive school environment.

Being the best version of ourselves at work

In our busy and competitive work lives, being the best version of ourselves has never been more important. It is not just about coming to work and 'doing our job' or 'climbing the career ladder'; it is also about growing and developing ourselves as people, feeling greater levels of satisfaction and being well-rounded.

Why does this matter so much when schools have traditionally been a place where students come to learn and educators go to educate? In today's fast-paced work environment with many highly important competing demands, the idea of being the best version of ourselves has gained significance – to grow as a person, to feel satisfied, to feel valued and respected, and to feel authentically aligned with our employer. This concept transcends achieving professional success – it plays to our wellbeing and our desire to remain in the work environment. But why is it so crucial to for us strive for this ideal at work?

Being our best self means that we remain true to ourselves: our values, our morals, our strengths and, ultimately, who we are as people. This in turn brings about a sense of meaning, purpose and happiness. When we experience these feelings at work we are more likely to experience the following outcomes:

- **Feel a greater sense of personal satisfaction:**
  - Putting forward our best effort
  - Being more engaged in continuous self-improvement
  - Experiencing a greater sense of accomplishment and pride
  - Developing our self-image
  - Boosting our confidence
  - Increasing our level of resilience when facing work-related challenges

- **Cultivate professional growth:**
  - Being committed to excellence
  - Seeking opportunities to expand our skillset
  - Taking on new challenges
  - Enhancing our capabilities

- **Build stronger connections:**
  - Improving our interpersonal skills as we communicate more effectively
  - Improving our ability to collaborate and work as part of a team
  - Creating a more supportive network
  - Fostering a more productive environment
  - Inspiring others

- **Enhance wellbeing and create a positive culture:**
  - Enhancing a sense of fulfillment and purpose
  - Reducing anxiety
  - Improving resilience
  - Fostering a culture of excellence and mutual support
  - Pursuing high standards and creating a positive, dynamic work environment where innovation thrives.

Being the best version of ourselves at work is not just about success. It is about increasing personal satisfaction, cultivating professional growth, building strong connections, enhancing wellbeing and creating a positive work culture. By being aware of who we are, committing to continuous self-improvement and striving for excellence, we not only enhance our own professional life but also contribute significantly to the success and wellbeing of our colleagues, students and the institution. The journey to being our best selves is a rewarding endeavour that can lead to a more fulfilling, balanced and successful career.

Reflection: Being your best self at work

Ask yourself the following questions:

- What are your character strengths? How are you able to use them at work?
- Do you see any of your character strengths becoming problematic at work?
- Does your workplace have barriers that restrict you from engaging your character strengths through your practice?
- When do you feel motivated at work? What activities are you doing?
- What goals would you like to achieve at work? How can you use your character strengths to achieve them?
- When work presents you with challenges, how can you engage your character strengths to work through them?
- What do you want your character strengths to say about you to others?

With your responses in mind, reflect on how you could increase your personal satisfaction, cultivate professional growth, build strong connections, enhance your wellbeing and create a positive work culture.

Ask yourself the following questions:

- Do I use my strengths to seek out opportunities for learning and personal growth?
- Do I use my strengths to communicate effectively and respectfully with others?
- What strengths do I need to employ so that I am open to feedback and willing to make improvements?

- What strengths do I need to use as I set and work towards achieving my goals?
- How do I use my strengths to contribute to establishing a supportive and collaborative work environment?
- Do I use the strength of gratitude to recognise and appreciate others' efforts?
- How do I engage my strengths to effectively balance my goals with the school's strategic direction?

Regularly asking yourself these questions can help you stay on track towards being the best version of yourself, both personally and professionally.

Building staff capacity

Building capacity is about helping people develop their skills and abilities, making it easier for staff to refine their craft, achieve their goals, face challenges and contribute to the overall growth of the institution.

In a school setting, building capacity could mean teachers learning new teaching methodologies or integrating advanced classroom technologies to improve student engagement and learning outcomes. It also encompasses the development of soft skills such as effective communication, time management and strategic thinking. These are essential for creating a productive and collaborative educational environment. Additionally, it involves regularly evaluating and enhancing the school's overall capabilities, such as administrative processes, resource allocation, curriculum distribution and support systems. This will ensure that the institution operates smoothly, efficiently and purposefully, ultimately benefiting both staff and students. Table 5 provides examples of ways to target specific focus areas.

Table 5: Examples of building staff capacity

Focus area	Description	Example
Teamwork and productivity	Sharing best practices and resources to tackle challenges and achieve shared goals.	Teachers collaborating and co-constructing curriculum plans and sharing classroom strategies.

Focus area	Description	Example
Innovation and creativity	Encouraging creative thinking and developing new ideas.	Developing interdisciplinary units of work to create authentic experiences for the students. This can include student-directed passion projects.
Strategic planning and decision-making	Anticipating problems and developing strategic plans for informed decision-making.	Being proactive and co-creating strategic plans for curriculum development or co-curricular activities.
Resilience and flexibility	Fostering continuous learning and professional development to handle changes effectively.	Actively engage and participate in professional learning communities (PLCs) to adapt to new pedagogies or educational standards.
Individual growth	Paying attention to and addressing strengths and growth areas to boost confidence and take on additional responsibilities.	Providing mentorship for improving classroom management skills or training for technological proficiency, encouraging teachers to inspire.
Meeting the school community's needs	Allocating resources to match school requirements for timely completion of set goals.	Being proactive with school events, parent-teacher interviews and service programs to meet the needs of the school and the wider community.

For leaders, knowing their staff is crucial in this process. Understanding individual strengths, areas for growth and professional goals allows leaders to tailor their capacity-building efforts to meet the specific needs of their team. By building strong relationships and maintaining open communication, leaders can create personalised development plans that are more effective and meaningful. Table 6 provides some suggested development initiatives.

Table 6: Suggested development initiatives

Initiative	Explanation	Example in a school setting
Leadership development programs	Develop skills in strategic thinking, decision-making and team management at various leadership levels within your school's context.	Developing teachers for future leadership roles through leadership courses that focus on personal and professional growth, e.g. challenging conversations.
Interactive workshops	Teach new skills and ways of thinking through structured learning activities.	Organising planned activities for teachers to learn new educational technologies or innovative teaching methods.
Mentoring partnerships	Involve pairing staff for growth and development. This does not have to be based on 'years of experience' but rather what each staff member brings to the school.	Pairing teachers for guidance and growth on curriculum, pedagogy, technology, classroom management, wellbeing practices and career development.
Taskforces	Identify and improve areas within school – administrative processes, curriculum planning, wellbeing strategies and so on – to make them more efficient and effective.	Creating a taskforce to address a particular issues. For example, curriculum documentation: introduce collaborative planning sessions and a digital platform for sharing lesson plans and resources to streamline tasks. This promotes teamwork and a cohesive educational experience.

A good capacity-building strategy empowers teachers and staff to take charge of their professional growth. They can identify areas for improvement, set goals and create plans to achieve them. This leads to a more effective and supportive educational environment. When leaders are actively involved and aware of their staff's needs, capacity-building efforts are significantly more impactful, fostering a culture of continuous improvement and collaboration.

Table 7 outlines some of the benefits of building staff capacity.

Table 7: Benefits of building staff capacity

Benefit	Explanation	Example in a school setting
Improved student outcomes	Qualified teachers provide higher-quality education.	Teachers learning new strategies to better engage students and improve academic performance.
Feeling valued and fulfilled	Supported staff with professional growth opportunities are more satisfied and may be less likely to leave the organisation and profession.	Providing bespoke professional development and mentorship for staff to grow their capabilities.
Improved flexibility and adaptability	Staff who continuously improve their skills and knowledge are likely to be better equipped to handle changes in the educational landscape.	Staff who regularly engage in professional development usually adapt to changes in teaching pedagogy, updated curricula or technological advancements in education more quickly and effectively, ensuring that the school remains current and effective in providing quality education. Staff reflect on their professional growth, map their learning balance, set goals, and share best practices, fostering a culture of continuous improvement through peer discussions and follow-ups.

Benefit	Explanation	Example in a school setting
Effective team dynamics	Capacity-building fosters a collaborative environment.	Professional learning communities (PLCs) are a powerful tool for improving teaching practices and student outcomes. By fostering collaboration, reflective practice and continuous improvement, PLCs help create a supportive and effective educational environment, while providing opportunities for staff to demonstrate their expertise in specific areas.
Effective leadership preparation	Developing staff capacity helps prepare them for future leadership positions.	Leadership training for teachers to help them understand their potential, capabilities and growth points to prepare for moving into leadership positions.
Improved problem-solving and innovation	Well-equipped staff are better at identifying and solving problems creatively.	Continuous professional development leading to innovative teaching methods that improve student engagement.

Fostering connection

A feeling of connection is absolutely crucial in any work environment, and schools are no exception. They are no longer just places where teachers go to teach lessons; they have become communities where teachers, administrators and support staff come together to help students grow. There is substantial research showing that when school staff feel connected and work well together there is a positive effect on student accomplishment and wellbeing.

The importance of connection is illustrated in the book *TomorrowMind* by Gabriella Rosen Kellerman and Martin Seligman (2023). The authors emphasise the importance of social connections in the workplace, arguing that strong relationships among colleagues lead to greater resilience, collaboration and overall wellbeing. Kellerman and Seligman suggest that fostering a sense of community and support in professional settings is crucial for helping staff navigate the uncertainties and challenges of the modern world. They emphasise the importance of diverse perspectives and inclusive environments in fostering resilience, innovation and overall organisational success – all of which are underpinned by being connected through trust and cohesion.

Schools are diverse in that they generally serve students from a range of backgrounds, each with unique needs and learning styles. Effective collaboration and communication among staff members allows them to pool resources and expertise, thereby ensuring no student is left behind and everyone receives the support they need. Consistent and open communication keeps everyone on the same page, enabling teachers to share successful strategies and seek advice on challenges, leading to a unified teaching approach.

This collaborative environment provides students with holistic support, addressing not just academic needs but also their social, emotional and behavioural needs. When educators work together, they create a cohesive learning environment where students experience consistent expectations and teaching methods across different classes, year levels and subjects. This consistency helps students feel more secure and understood, which is critical for their overall development.

Moreover, students who see their teachers and school staff working together respectfully and supportively are more likely to feel safe and valued. This positive modelling of relationships teaches students about cooperation, conflict resolution and the importance of community. When students feel safe and supported, they are more likely to engage in their learning, participate actively in class, take risks in their learning and develop a deeper interest in their studies. This engagement is a key predictor of academic success, leading to better academic performance.

Why does connection make a difference?

When staff feel connected at work it isn't just a nice 'bonus' – it is essential for them to feel fulfilled in what they do. In schools, this means feeling like they are part of a team where they are valued and understood by their colleagues. When they feel this way, it keeps everyone motivated and helps them deal with the challenges of teaching without burning out.

Why does working together lead to success?

Schools thrive on teamwork. Teachers collaborate on lesson plans, share ideas and support each other to help all students succeed. When there is a strong sense of connection among staff, it makes communication easier and teamwork more effective. This collaboration leads to better teaching practices, stronger support systems for students and a more unified approach to achieving the school's goals.

Why is creating a positive school culture important?

A positive school culture is crucial for students and staff alike. When teachers feel connected to their colleagues, it creates an atmosphere of respect and support that students can feel. This positive environment helps students learn better and feel safer and happier at school.

How does being connected help students succeed?

The connection among staff directly impacts student success. When staff work well together, they can meet students' diverse needs more effectively. Good communication and shared strategies mean students get a better overall education. Additionally, when students see their teachers working together and supporting each other, it sets a great example and encourages them to do their best.

Friend expert Dana Kerford (2018) states: 'Quality relationships are based in trust and respect and we feel good when we're with that person. We feel like we can be ourselves, we have fun.'

Tips for building connections

- **Build relationships:** Take time for team-building activities and professional development opportunities that let staff get to know each other better. Create opportunities to celebrate with staff.
- **Keep talking:** Regular meetings and informal chats help keep communication open and make sure everyone is on the same page. Propose topics of discussion to encourage everyone to explore their thoughts and feelings on how their goals and the school's strategic plan are aligning.

- **Support each other:** Mentorship programs and recognition for hard work help build a supportive community. Build in opportunities for staff sharing and celebrations of accomplishments.
- **Share the load:** Involve as many people as possible in decision-making through committees and working parties so everyone feels invested in the school's success.

Feeling connected at work isn't just important for how we feel – it is essential for the success of our school community. When we build strong connections among staff, we create an environment where everyone feels valued and supported. This leads to better teamwork, a positive school culture and, ultimately, better outcomes for our students. So let's invest in building those connections and making our school a place where everyone can thrive.

Activity: A simple way to build staff connection

Have each staff member share:
- A photo(s) of something that brings them joy
- A song that they love.

Combine the photos and snippets of the songs using an app such as MovieMaker or iMovie, and play this at the start of your staff meetings. A three or four minute video works wonders to energise and focus staff while at the same time developing understanding about what makes their colleagues happy.

Creating a feedback culture based on trust

A common theme that has been and will continue to be discussed in this book is trust. Trust is fundamental when it comes to developing relationships – both personally and professionally. In a school setting, fostering a safe and supportive environment where students, teachers and staff feel valued and respected means that community members (staff, students and parents) are likely to engage openly and collaboratively, support each other's growth and contribute to a stronger, cohesive environment.

One way to build trust is through the development of a feedback culture. This is where students and staff feel safe and encouraged to give and receive feedback without fear of any negative consequences. This culture can thrive in classrooms and throughout the school when open communication is valued. This level of open communication is founded on the basis of respect, involving the practice of interacting with others in a considerate and kind manner that displays regard for their feelings and perspectives. This doesn't mean everyone has to agree with others' perspectives, but rather that they engage in active listening, speak politely and acknowledge different perspectives so that everyone feels valued and understood. By showing empathy and understanding, we demonstrate that we care about others' feelings and opinions. Consistently following through on promises and being honest also strengthens trust, while at the same time establishing an understanding that having different opinions can lead to positive growth.

In a school setting, this means students and staff communicate openly and respectfully, creating an environment where everyone feels safe, heard and valued. This foundation of respectful communication helps build strong and trusting relationships throughout the school community.

This idea is supported by the work of Brené Brown, who explores the development of a feedback culture in her books, particularly through her extensive work on vulnerability, courage and leadership. Brown advocates for creating environments where open, honest and compassionate feedback is the norm. In *Dare to Lead* (2018), Brown highlights the need for clear, direct communication to foster trust and growth. Brown believes that feedback should be grounded in empathy and delivered in a way that respects the receiver's dignity. Brown also stresses the importance of being vulnerable when giving and receiving feedback, as it requires courage to address difficult truths and navigate the discomfort of these conversations. Brown (2018) writes that 'Feedback thrives in cultures where the goal is not getting comfortable with hard conversations but normalising discomfort'. By cultivating a culture where feedback is seen as a tool for development rather than criticism, Brown argues that individuals and teams can achieve greater innovation, connection and overall success.

To establish this culture, it is important to have guidelines to ensure feedback is constructive, to avoid only harsh criticism or purely positive comments. Building this culture takes time, effort and regular adjustments. A school environment that has a culture of feedback as part of everyday interactions (not just as part of an appraisal process) will discover many benefits. But first, you will need to work to:

- **Create habits of giving and receiving feedback:**
  - As a regular daily practice, encourage discussion about what has gone well and what could be modified for improvement next time.
  - Maintain a focus on a growth mindset.
- **Foster a psychologically safe and supportive environment:**
  - Where staff feel safe to share their thoughts and opinions, even if they differ from the leaders.
  - Where the focus of feedback is on actions and not on personal traits.
  - Where leaders lead by example – hearing feedback without becoming defensive.
- **Provide training and resources for giving and receiving feedback:**
  - Professional development on how to give and receive feedback can provide clear language guidelines and examples of how to frame your feedback so emphasis is placed on the action or process and not the person.
- **Provide opportunities for open and honest discussions:**
  - Have regular meetings where staff voices can be heard and valued – what is working well and what opportunities are there for growth?
  - Allocate a facilitator so that the discussion remains focused and productive.
- **Set clear expectations:**
  - Provide clear guidelines around how feedback should be given and why it is important.
  - Link these back to personal and professional goals that have been set.

As a result of this established trust and respect, you should be able to notice the following benefits:

- **Enhanced learning and flexibility**: Immediate feedback provides continuous learning opportunities for both students and teachers. This helps everyone grow, improve and quickly adapt, making the teaching and learning processes more effective by reinforcing new skills and improving on required areas of growth. Teams accustomed to regular feedback can adapt more easily to changing educational needs and strategies, ensuring the school remains dynamic and responsive.

- **Working together for increased alignment**: Feedback helps staff and students understand how their efforts contribute to school goals, creating a sense of purpose. This ensures everyone works towards the same objectives, improving overall performance. Regular feedback also allows for setting and tracking smaller, achievable goals, boosting success and fostering a high-performing school culture – which benefits both academic results and wellbeing.

- **Better communication and relationships**: Regular feedback keeps the lines of communication open between the various members of the school community. This building of trust helps reduce stress as feedback happens regularly rather than only during formal reviews – strengthening relationships and creating a supportive, team-oriented school culture.

- **Engagement and development of school members**: Feedback helps staff and students grow and succeed by promoting a growth mindset, boosting engagement and commitment, while making everyone feel valued and motivated.

- **Improved collaboration and school culture:** Consistent feedback encourages peer support and teamwork, creating an environment where teachers help each other improve and achieve common goals. A robust feedback culture encourages everyone to give and receive feedback, leveraging diverse perspectives to build a high-performing school culture. Concerns are addressed promptly and constructively, helping teams collaborate more effectively to identify solutions and overcome obstacles.

Feedback questions for staff

Following are some open-ended questions to gather feedback on staff engagement, recognition, support, communication, growth and organisational values:

- How do you feel about your role within the school and the connection you have with your students?

- In what ways do you feel recognised and appreciated for your contributions to the school?
- What can we do to best support your professional growth and development as an educator/employee?
- How comfortable are you expressing your opinions and ideas within the school? What could improve this?
- What opportunities for growth and career development have you found most beneficial? What additional support would you like from the school to maximise your growth?
- How well do you feel the school prioritises diversity, equity and inclusion, and what opportunities are there for further growth?
- Are there any challenges or obstacles you're facing in your role that we can assist with?
- How would you describe the overall communication within the school, and what changes would enhance it?

CHAPTER 4

FLOURISHING THROUGH PURPOSE AND FORGIVENESS

Focusing on You

Nurture your wellbeing, find your purpose, understand your 'why' and embrace forgiveness to flourish as an educator.

'Do you have a minute?' We all know the sound of those wonderful words that we hear working in an educational institution. It doesn't matter if you work in the front office, in maintenance, in support services, in the classroom or in leadership – it is these words that we all constantly hear. Since most people who choose to work in a school environment are caring and giving people, the answer we give more often than not is 'Yes.' But each time we say 'yes', we add an extra layer to our ever-growing workload.

Whether we're educators and support staff, we have so much to deal with. There are the emails, parent meetings, classroom displays, emails, planning, assessing, yard duties, emails, reports, student counselling, refereeing of behaviour, emails, staff meetings, hub groups, data collection, research, and did I say emails? I'm sure you would be able to add many other duties to this list.

When all of these demands are occurring at the same time that you are conducting your primary duties (which, if you're an educator, is teaching – which is a task that wasn't on that list), how are you going to make sure that you look after your own wellbeing, both professionally and personally?

So, let's start with you! How well do you know yourself? How easily can you articulate what makes you *you*, as a person and as an educator? What most people find here is that there is often tension between who we are and who we want to be.

Reflection: What makes you *you*?

Fill in the table below to gain a clearer picture of what makes you *you*.

About you	What does this look like outside of school?	What does this look like inside of school?
Think of the things that matter most to you. Name five of the most significant.		
We all have ideas on how we want to be remembered. How would you?		

About you	What does this look like outside of school?	What does this look like inside of school?
Identify three ways that you look after your physical wellbeing.		
Identify three ways that you look after your emotional/ psychological wellbeing.		
What are three words you would use to describe yourself?		

Focus on what you can control

One area of our wellbeing that is often overlooked is the emphasis and emotion we place on things that are out of our control. Understanding what is within your control versus what is out of your control is a vital aspect of maintaining your wellbeing, particularly in a school context where significant external factors such as policies, strategic direction and students' home lives are beyond your control. What is within your control are your actions, thoughts, reactions, and the effort you put into the tasks and duties you are assigned. You have the power to manage your time, set boundaries and choose how you respond to various situations. By focusing on what you can control, you work to reduce your levels of stress, improve your mental health and increase your resilience. Accepting and letting go of what you cannot control allows you to conserve energy and maintain a positive perspective.

Activity: Your realm of control

Create a list of activities and tasks undertaken in your teams/classes/school and work through how they make you feel, how you respond to them and what this might look like. See the example in the table below.

	Example 1	Example 2	Your example
Things out of my control	Reports Nationally Consistent Collection of Data (NCCD) evidence Changes in curriculum	How something makes me feel	
What I can control	How I approach the many things I need to do	How I respond How long I choose to feel this way before moving on	
What this might look like	Breaking down tasks over time so they don't build up	Stopping and thinking about the PMIs (Plus, Minus, Interesting) of the situation	
How these make you feel	Anxious, stressed about workload	Overwhelmed, frustrated or powerless	
Strategies to overcome negative thoughts	Instead of 'This workload is too much,' reframe it to 'I can break this down and tackle it step by step' Self-compassion – perfection isn't necessary; progress matters	Pause, reflect and reframe your thoughts Accept what you can and can't control	

Knowing what is in or out of your control fundamentally helps you to boost your wellbeing and plan more effectively. It enables the goals you set for yourself to be more focused on what is in your realm of control (such as your actions, your efforts and your responses) and are, therefore, more likely to be achieved. In turn, this helps promote and maintain motivation, reduce frustration (from uncontrollable variables) and helps build a more positive outlook. Aligning your goals with what you can influence creates a clear path to achievement that reinforces self-confidence and your overall mental health.

Teachers (and schools) frequently establish performance-oriented goals, but sometimes forget to prioritise goals that enhance their overall wellbeing. Significant research has revealed that individuals who prioritise their wellbeing often achieve higher performance levels. Caroline Adams Miller has extensively explored the connection between goal-setting and wellbeing in her work. In her book *Creating Your Best Life*, written with Dr Michael Frisch (2009), Miller delves into how setting and achieving goals can significantly enhance happiness and overall life satisfaction. She emphasises that setting meaningful goals aligned with personal values and strengths plays a crucial role in improving your overall wellbeing.

One of the most popular and practical frameworks for setting goals with clear objectives is SMART goals: specific (clear and precise), measurable (able to track progress), achievable (realistic and doable), relevant (related to what matters) and timely (with a set deadline). Following these guidelines helps make sure goals are well-defined and increases the chances of you reaching them. It is about setting goals that are clear, doable, and connected to what's important to you, with a clear timeline for getting them done. SMART goals help keep you focused and motivated as you work towards achieving them.

The framework I have chosen to adopt are WOOP goals: wish (something you'd like to achieve), outcome (how you will feel when your goal is achieved), obstacle (what might prevent you from achieving your goal) and plan (devise strategies to help overcome the obstacles). WOOP goals offer several advantages. They:

- Provide clarity and focus by helping you articulate your wish and define the specific outcome you want to achieve.
- Encourage setting goals that are realistic and achievable. By identifying potential obstacles, you can realistically assess what might

prevent achievement and how to overcome these challenges. This realism ensures that goals are not overly ambitious or impossible to achieve.
- Emphasise actionable planning where you develop concrete steps to overcome obstacles.
- Increase your level of motivation by linking your aspirations to tangible outcomes and practical actions.
- Promote flexibility and resilience by encouraging agile plans knowing that challenges will get in the way of achieving your desired outcomes.

Goal-setting plays an important role in establishing and maintaining self-care rituals that will lead to improved habits. By setting specific goals, such as committing to daily 'mindful moments', or practising daily gratitude through 'what went wells', you create a framework for repeated behaviour that may become ingrained habits and contribute significantly to your overall wellbeing.

When thinking of your wellbeing goals, focus on who you want to be. In chapter 3, I spoke about the benefits of being the best version of yourself. To be this person, why not write your 'to be' list? Set this as part of your goals. Far too often our days are consumed with our to-do lists where we focus on tasks or activities that just needs to be *done*. In doing this we neglect the more valuable question of who we are trying to be. Imagine if you carefully planned your goals around self-care and becoming the person you want to be.

Remember, when it comes to self-care, it is important to practise what you preach. Some of the following phrases are things you may commonly say to others. But how often do you apply them to yourself? Make sure you:

- Are taking time to savour, to be present in the moment
- Separate personal from task-oriented criticism
- Set achievable goals – with plans for when obstacles get in your way
- Maintain hope
- Demonstrate gratitude
- Focus on your relationships
- Actively be the best possible you.

Reflection: Setting your wellbeing goals

Set your wellbeing goals by asking yourself:
- How do I want to regulate my emotions?
- What do I need to do to maintain healthy relationships?
- How can I balance my perspective to maintain helpful thoughts?
- What daily habit could I develop around self-care?
- How can I be aware of the 'now' so I can savour the moment?

Finding meaning and purpose

We have already established how busy our daily lives have become, particularly when we work in a school. We know it is easy to get caught up in routines and activities that drive us to lose sight of the bigger picture: our purpose. We find ourselves either forgetting or moving away from our purpose – the reasons behind choosing to be who we are or to do what we do. In a school environment, if has never been more important than now to rediscover and hold on to the 'why' – the meaning and purpose behind choosing to be in education.

Understanding meaning and purpose

People often believe the terms 'meaning' and 'purpose' mean the same thing. However, delving a bit deeper into the two terms shows they have different shades of meaning. *Meaning* is about the importance we attach to our experiences and the understanding we get from them. *Purpose*, on the other hand, is more about our direction and goals in life – what we aim to achieve or contribute.

Building on his work on optimism, motivation and character, Martin Seligman published his 2011 book *Flourish: A Visionary New Understanding of Happiness and Well-being*. This book outlines the five key elements of the PERMA model – positive emotion, engagement, relationships, meaning and achievement – as essential components of wellbeing. Seligman says:

> *Meaning comes from belonging to and serving something beyond yourself and from developing the best within you. This element of wellbeing, meaning, is ineluctably subjective. We all have our own visions of what gives life purpose.*

Having a sense of meaning and purpose is linked to many benefits, including better psychological and physical health, more resilience and greater life satisfaction. People who have a strong sense of purpose are likely to be more motivated and focused, and better able to bounce back from tough times.

When we transfer this concept into a school environment, we see that our values, passions, strengths, goals, sense of belonging and flexibility all play a significant role in establishing our own meaning and purpose within our school environment.

What are your values?

Our values guide our behaviour and the decisions we make. Values are our core beliefs and are fundamental to our identity, and to what can ultimately bring us joy.

How often have you stopped to ask yourself about your values? What qualities do you admire in others? What principles do you hold dear? When do you feel your most authentic and true to yourself?

What are your passions?

What are the things that excite you the most? Your passions are activities or causes that energise you. Your passions will most likely align with your values and help you find a greater sense of fulfillment, bringing you increased levels of joy. We have all experienced occasions where we have lost track of time, where we have become totally absorbed in an event or activity and feel deeply focused with high levels of enjoyment. This is often referred to a being in 'flow' – a concept named by Mihaly Csikszentmihalyi. This happens when the challenge of the activity or event matches your skills, interests and being perfectly, causing you to lose track of time and feel naturally motivated.

Think about instances where you have lost track of time. What topics do you love to learn about? What kind of work or hobbies make you feel most engaged and alive?

What are your strengths?

Your strengths can refer to both character strengths, and your talents and skills. They can be where you are demonstrating your abilities that come naturally to you, where you are making a significant impact or where you are able to act in a way that is aligned with your character strengths and your authentic self.

Think about what you do that you feel naturally good at, or what others might ask you to help them with. When have you felt most effective? When have you been able to act in a way that has felt naturally you?

What vision do you have for your life?

When you think about your ideal future, what would you like to accomplish? What is the legacy you would like to leave behind? How would you like others to remember you?

The answers to these questions can help you plan both your short and long-term goals and aspirations and help you achieve them. Using either SMART or WOOP goals, you can break your vision down into achievable steps that will help you build momentum over time.

How do you find purpose and fulfillment?

When you are mindful you stay in the moment and pay attention to your thoughts, feelings and what is around you. You connect with yourself and uncover what really matters to you. What might you do to help you be in the present? Spending time with people who support and inspire you benefits your ability to form flourishing relationships. What can you do to build connections and a sense of community in your environment?

Our lives are constantly evolving, demonstrating the importance of developing our ability to adapt and be flexible. How do you allow yourself to be open to new experiences? As you grow older, your sense of purpose can shift, and it becomes up to you whether or not you embrace challenges as opportunities to grow. If you want to follow your dreams, the goals you've set or the values that you hold, you may be faced with some tough decisions, or the feelings of doubt or fear. Trust in yourself and celebrate the small steps of progress you make along the way, using your connections for support. It is these experiences that will, over time, help you discover your purpose.

Making a positive impact

When we engage in work that benefits others' wellbeing this can provide us with a profound sense of purpose and personal satisfaction. As educators, we are actively involved in activities that support our students' physical, emotional and psychological wellbeing, which we know can be highly rewarding. This goes beyond teaching the curriculum; it's about creating a supportive and nurturing classroom environment. When we see the positive impact of our efforts on students' growth and development, we feel a greater sense of meaning, motivation and purpose. This, in turn, leads to significant personal fulfillment and happiness.

Ask yourself:

- How do you feel when you see the positive impact of your work on others?
- How does witnessing your students' growth and development influence your motivation and sense of job satisfaction?
- What role do you believe personal satisfaction plays in your overall effectiveness as a teacher?
- What do you do to stay motivated and passionate about teaching, even during challenging times?

What is your 'why'?

In addition to knowing our meaning and purpose, understanding our 'why' is crucial to our wellbeing, particularly in our work environment. 'Why' statements increase our awareness of and focus on our higher purpose.

Simon Sinek, an ethnographer who studies the behaviours and communication patterns of impactful individuals and organisations, is well-known for his TED Talk on the concept of 'why'. He famously says: 'People don't buy what you do; they buy why you do it, and what you do simply proves what you believe.' Sinek is all about making a world where people wake up inspired, feel secure and end their day fulfilled by their work. He really emphasises finding your 'why' – that deep, meaningful purpose that guides and fulfills you.

What is a 'why' statement?

A 'why' statement helps you understand and express your fundamental purpose, cause or belief. It helps you clarify what motivates you beyond mere goal-setting. As educators, it defines the deeper significance that lies beyond our role in education and guides our efforts to inspire, educate and empower students towards success and personal growth. A 'why' statement can act as a guiding principle to shape our teaching philosophy and classroom practices.

Crafting your 'why' statement

To start crafting your 'why' statement, begin by reflecting on your core beliefs and values. What is it that truly motivates and inspires you beyond your immediate goals or achievements? Have in mind the key moments that have shaped your values and beliefs. As you break down and refine these thoughts, aim for clarity and authenticity in expressing your 'why' so that it not only defines your personal or professional aspirations but also helps guide your actions.

Ask yourself:

- When am I at my best or worst?
- What am I passionate about?
- When do I feel most energised?
- What is the core purpose of my role, and why does it matter?
- What am I doing when I feel I'm in flow?

Your answers to these questions will help you identify key themes and words that evoke an emotional response, helping you look for recurring ideas and common threads. Group similar themes together to highlight your core motivations and values. Use these insights to craft a meaningful and authentic 'why' statement that deeply resonates with you.

Sinek says that a strong 'why' statement should be clear and inspiring, and feel genuine. It should guide how you make choices and act, both in your personal life and at work. He provides a simple format for us to use to draft our statements:

To [contribution] so that [impact].

For example:

To empower my students so they can discover and fulfil their potential.

When we know our 'why', and the 'why' of our work environments, this can lead to more conversation that in turn builds trust and authenticity. When your personal 'why' aligns with your career 'why' it promotes harmony and a greater sense of balance between your personal and professional life. It helps you maintain a clear sense of purpose that can effectively guide your decisions and help you prioritise meaningful and fulfilling opportunities.

As educators we wear many 'hats' – all of thich are tangible and reflect things that need to be done. However, they are all disconnected when we look at them as *what* we have to do or *how* we have to do them.

But imagine if we shift the focus to *why* we do each task (see table 8)? Then each of these tasks becomes more connected as they are all helping us work towards achieving the same goal.

Table 8: How and what versus why

How and what?	Why?
How am I going to design this lesson? →	Why am I going to design this lesson?
How should I assess this assignment? →	Why should I assess this assignment?
How do I want to contact this parent? →	Why do I want to contact this parent?

If we aim to put the *why* before the *how* and the *what* we will strive to find purpose, clarity and alignment which can lead to meaningful change.

Activity: School-wide 'why' statements

To help you understand how your 'why' statement aligns with others within the school, or with the school itself based on its context, ask these questions:

- Why do we do what we do?
- What is our core business?
- Why does our school exist?
- Why do we come to school/work every day?

Can you develop a combined statement that aligns each other's beliefs? What are the common features? Are there differences?

Looking after our wellbeing through forgiveness

Forgiveness is often seen as a noble quality: something to aim for when someone has wronged us. But forgiveness is more than just a choice; it is an essential component of our overall wellbeing. Forgiveness impacts our psychological, emotional and physical health by helping us let go of resentment and move towards fostering stronger relationships, ultimately achieving a deeper sense of peace and fulfillment.

For educators, practising forgiveness can not only transform our lives but also create a healthier school environment, leading to happier interactions and a more positive atmosphere for everyone.

Understanding forgiveness

Forgiveness is often seen as something we do for others. However, we now know that the act of forgiveness has a significant wellbeing benefit for ourselves.

Forgiveness means choosing to let go of anger or bitterness towards someone who has hurt you. It is about finding peace for yourself, not necessarily excusing or forgetting what has happened. This shift from anger to understanding can significantly improve your wellbeing by helping you reclaim your own sense of peace and emotional balance.

Forgiveness is an active, deliberate decision to put aside feelings of resentment towards someone who may have been unfair, hurtful or committed a wrong against you. It doesn't mean simply accepting what has happened or that you stop being angry. Rather, it is about a process of adjusting your feelings and behaviour so that you can express compassion, generosity and even a level of understanding towards the person who has wronged you. By doing this, we aim to release any form of resentment or anger that we are harbouring – ultimately working to lift our mood, increase our levels of optimism, rebalance our emotions and begin the process of moving forward.

Through forgiveness, we learn to let go of negative emotions and shift our focus towards the more positive ones, resulting in the building of stronger relationships. We learn empathy and compassion, both of which are crucial if we are to maintain or establish a supportive and understanding environment. As we move the negative emotions towards the positive, we work to reduce our levels of stress and anxiety – the result of which can potentially play out in our physical health through the lowering of blood pressure and the building of a stronger immune system. Studies have shown the connection between forgiveness and hope where individuals move forward and find new possibilities (hope), countering despair.

Forgiveness is a deeply personal journey. It involves acknowledging and accepting the past while working through your emotions. This often requires your time and inward thought.

While seeming obvious, one of the most effective methods to help process forgiveness is to document your feelings and experiences (articulating your emotions) – allowing reflection over time, to lead to greater self-awareness, and an increased sense of clarity and relief. The aim of this is to notice a shift in your perspective, helping you move towards forgiveness and emotional healing.

Ultimately, forgiveness brings a sense of peace and fulfillment, allowing you to live more fully in the present and look forward to the future with hope and positivity. By choosing to forgive, you free yourself from the past and open the door to a happier, healthier life.

As educators, we may be triggered into anger or hurt as a result of conflict with a colleague, student or parent. Forgiveness in these circumstances offers numerous benefits such as enhancing our psychological, emotional and spiritual wellbeing. The reduction of stress and anxiety, the promotion of a calmer state of mind and the lowering of depressive symptoms all work together to help educators maintain a positive attitude and handle challenging situations more effectively. In addition, stronger relationships with colleagues, students and the wider community all combine to form a supportive classroom and school ethos where empathy, compassion and the ability to overcome any human limitations are central to maintaining an inclusive school culture.

Practical ways to promote forgiveness

- **Acknowledge and validate the feelings of hurt:** Recognise the level of anger or discomfort the event has triggered for you.
- **Seek a sense of empathy:** Understanding, or trying to see someone else's perspective, doesn't mean that their behaviour is excused. Rather, it can help to provide additional contextual information for your consideration. This is valuable when working with students to better resolve any behavioural or academic challenges they may face.

- **Find support in others:** Remember that it is okay to speak with someone for guidance and support – a friend, a manager a counsellor.
- **Make a deliberate choice:** Forgiveness is a decision – an active choice. You must be willing to let go of any resentment to be able to move forward. In essence, this decision leads to a more positive environment.
- **Act to demonstrate forgiveness:** What will you do to reinforce that you are able to let go and move forward? Some people choose to write it down (via a letter or email), while others prefer to speak openly with the person they are forgiving.
- **Think of the now:** When our focus is on the past, we struggle to find ways to move forward. Having hope and thinking about how the present time will shape your future helps re-engage positive integrations and relationships.

CHAPTER 5
PLANNING A WHOLE-SCHOOL APPROACH
Guiding Wellbeing

Adopt a whole-school approach to wellbeing and reap the benefits of a balanced strategy. Start by gaining clarity, and conduct a wellbeing audit to guide your journey.

It is no secret that the successful implementation of any approach in a school is best done when it is in context and it encompasses all aspects of school life. The following statements, from various states across Australia, demonstrate how, in recent years, educators and policymakers have increasingly recognised the critical role that schools play in promoting a holistic approach to student wellbeing:

> *Learning and wellbeing are closely linked. Children and young people with good wellbeing are more engaged and successful learners. Likewise, gaining a good education is a key contributor to positive lifelong wellbeing outcomes.*
>
> – Department for Education, South Australia

> *A vision for learning and wellbeing helps teachers and school leaders to create a unified set of values and beliefs which drive the development of a high-performing and inclusive teaching culture. It creates the foundation for success and a narrative for change.*
>
> – Victorian Department of Education

> *Wellbeing and learning are inextricably linked and research shows that effective, evidence-based wellbeing initiatives and strategies enhance student learning.*
>
> – NSW Department of Education

> *We know that a supportive environment that combines a focus on wellbeing with a focus on learning is optimal – without one, the other will not happen.*
>
> – Queensland Department of Education

The concept of a whole-school approach to wellbeing embodies a comprehensive framework that acknowledges the interconnectedness of various factors that influence student wellbeing: relationships, connection and readiness for growth. Any wellbeing strategy should be designed to be multifaceted, authentic, strategic and intentional. This strategy has to become part of the school's fabric – where all members of the community live and breathe it. The term 'whole school' must reference everyone within the school community: students, teachers, leaders, support staff, volunteers and governing bodies.

A whole-school approach should have as its focus a purpose to make the school a healthier, safer and thriving place for students to learn and develop. Schools should be purposeful and intentional in their attempts to create positive emotions, engagement, relationships, meaning and purpose and accomplishment (PERMA), which, as we've discussed, are essential to living a flourishing life.

A whole-school approach to wellbeing is grounded in the understanding that wellbeing is influenced by multiple factors, including school culture, policies, practices and the physical environment. A whole-school approach should not sit outside the culture, ethos or learning direction of the school.

A whole-school approach incorporates the following principles:

- **Supporting everyone equally:** The whole-school approach ensures that all students and educators receive comprehensive support across various aspects of school life. This means addressing multiple needs simultaneously to benefit the entire school community.
- **Promoting consistency:** By focusing efforts on a common goal, a whole-school approach fosters consistency in practices and expectations. This helps create a unified and predictable environment which enhances effectiveness and understanding.
- **Encouraging collaboration:** Emphasising teamwork among students, teachers, parents and other key school community members, a whole-school approach embraces a collective effort to achieve a shared purpose and goals. Collaboration allows for the pooling of resources, expertise and ideas, leading to more impactful initiatives.
- **Optimising resource utilisation:** Through a coordinated approach to planning and resource allocation, schools are able to capitalise on the resources available to them, including human and financial, thus gaining maximum benefit.
- **Cultivating positive change:** A whole-school approach facilitates a cultural shift within educational institutions by embedding new practices, values and norms. It is this process that begins to encourage positive changes in behaviours and attitudes that build long-term institutional change.
- **Building sustainability:** By integrating interventions into the fabric of the school community, a whole-school approach promotes sustainability in that it establishes enduring practices that continue over time rather than relying on short-term fixes.
- **Prioritising holistic development:** Recognising that student growth is multidimensional, a whole-school approach makes holistic development a priority. By not only addressing academic needs, this

approach caters to the social, emotional and physical wellbeing of school community members.
- **Advocating for equity and inclusion:** A fundamental aspect of a whole-school approach is the promotion of equity and inclusivity. By tackling structural obstacles and inequalities, schools strive to ensure that all students are provided equal opportunities to succeed.
- **Informing decision-making:** An integral process in a whole-school approach is to carefully collect, analyse and utilise data to inform decision-making. Contextual, relevant information enables schools to make evidence-based decisions that drive continuous improvement.
- **Fostering positive school culture:** Through collaborative efforts and shared goals the whole-school approach contributes to the development of a positive school culture characterised by mutual respect, trust and support. This supportive environment is beneficial in promoting academic success, positive behaviour, strong relationships and emotional wellbeing among students and staff while promoting diversity and inclusion.

When we consider a whole-school approach through a wellbeing lens, it's clear that wellbeing should be 'taught' explicitly as well as 'caught' through implicit interactions and experiences within the school context. According to Quinlan and Hone (2020), 'Whole school wellbeing change requires attention to every level of the school's operations for students and staff: from enrolment and induction through reporting, reviews, curricula, disciplinary processes, awards systems, timetabling, assessment and many more.'

Reflection: A whole-school approach to wellbeing

When you're drilling down the implementation of a whole-school approach to wellbeing, there are practical steps to take. An important lesson to learn is that one size does not fit all. There are no 'correct' answers to the following questions; however, these should help you reflect on what might work for you.

What is your wellbeing policy?

Develop a clear wellbeing policy that includes a very clear definition of what wellbeing is in your context. This becomes the definition from which all policies, understandings, interactions and activities stem. It also sets out a clear purpose of what you want to achieve.

What will your staff need?

Professional development and upskilling staff will be vital in the successful implementation of the whole-school approach. It is important to start with the staff and support them to develop a better understanding of self. This helps provide greater clarity around their personal wellbeing and how it is impacted at various times, while providing tools to employ to increase levels of wellbeing. This sets a clear understanding of the purpose and benefits of utilising the various desired strategies with the student community.

Who are your champions?

One person cannot do this alone. Every school has like-minded people who share similar passions. Begin working with them so they can help grow the desired culture.

How will it be woven through your curriculum?

Incorporating wellbeing education into the curriculum will equip students with crucial life skills such as emotional regulation, stress management, interpersonal communication and conflict resolution.

How will you engage your community?

Involving families and communities in the school's wellbeing agenda through parent education workshops, community events, and collaborative partnerships with local organisations helps provide greater clarity and opportunities for transference between home and school.

What will you do to cultivate a positive school culture?

Fostering an environment that values empathy, kindness, inclusivity and diversity through initiatives such as positive relationships campaigns, peer support programs and recognition of achievements are all ways to create authentic experiences that clearly identify and articulate the culture you wish to establish.

The benefits of a well-rounded approach

The evidence that students' wellbeing is central to their development and success continues to grow. A well-rounded approach means that we take into account all factors contributing to wellbeing. According to the Programme for International Student Assessment (PISA) in 2015, these factors can be categorised as psychological, physical, cognitive, social and material (Borgonovi & Pál, 2016).

Where a well-rounded approach is taken and education focuses on the whole child, this helps to provide opportunities to nurture and develop a diverse range of skills essential for holistic growth. They go beyond academics and focus on developing qualities such as passion to acquire knowledge, a positive mindset and intellectual curiosity. In addition they instil values of independence, community engagement, global perspectives and social conscience while at the same time promoting connection. In a nutshell, a well-rounded education is like providing children with a very big toolbox, knowing that not every tool can fix a problem, but that there are multiple options from which to choose. Schools are not just places for learning information – they serve to empower students to lead purposeful, impactful and flourishing lives.

Employing a well-rounded approach to wellbeing not only enhances connection, relevance and meaning for all members of the school community, it also fosters a sense of belonging and support that strengthens relationships and promotes overall wellbeing. It entails a proactive approach to personal growth and development, fostering resilience, adaptability and a broadened worldview. Taking this broad approach to how children learn and feel means understanding how their health and happiness – how they feel physically, emotionally and socially – affects how well they do in school. Again, the whole-child approach means we look at everything that affects the child's school life (even though schools can't control everything) – their learning, their emotions, their sense of belonging, the school environment, and how families and the community are involved. The ultimate aim of this is to:

- **Promote connections that are equitable and authentic:** Fostering engagement across the school community providing all members (students, staff and families) with a genuine sense of belonging and connection to the school's values, mission and strategic plan. Everyone in the school is actively involved in the education process, strengthening relationships, building trust and fostering a supportive environment where the community feels valued and respected.

- **Enhance meaning:** Engaging in collective efforts towards a shared goal cultivates a sense of purpose and meaning for everyone involved. Students, educators and families alike find deeper significance in

their contributions to the overall wellbeing and success of the school community, fostering a greater sense of fulfillment and satisfaction.
- **Be relevant and contextual:** By involving all stakeholders in decision-making processes and initiatives, a well-rounded approach ensures that the activities and programs implemented are relevant and meaningful to the diverse needs and interests of the school community. Creating bespoke programs to address specific challenges and opportunities make them more meaningful for everyone involved.

Helen Street (2018) sums up the latter point when she says:

We will best support wellbeing and self-determination in young people by creating school contexts that support autonomy, build mindfulness, nurturing intrinsic motivation, support a love of learning in young people, and normalise trusting and compassionate relationships in our school communities.

The outcomes you can expect to see with a well-rounded approach include:

- **Comprehensive growth:** A well-rounded approach ensures that students develop in all areas, not just academics. For example, classes that are transdisciplinary in their approach and are intentional with wellbeing goals offer multi-pronged opportunities for students to develop.
- **Academic excellence:** By addressing students' wellbeing needs alongside academic learning, schools can boost academic performance. For example, programs to help students manage stress and anxiety can improve their focus, leading to better academic outcomes.
- **Social and emotional skills:** Integrating wellbeing practices into teaching helps students develop vital social and emotional skills. For example, teachers might incorporate cooperative learning activities to promote teamwork and communication skills, thus engaging students to learn to negotiate and to accept wins and losses.
- **A positive school environment:** A well-rounded approach fosters a positive school culture where everyone feels valued and supported. Examples for schools might be to implement programs such as peer mentoring or restorative justice practices to promote inclusivity and address conflicts constructively.

- **Behavioural improvement:** Addressing students' social and emotional needs can reduce behavioural issues in the schoolyard and classroom. Examples of strategies and programs schools might implement include:
    - Positive behaviour interventions
    - Zones of Regulation
    - Friendology
    - You Can Do It!
    - Bounce Back!
- **Improved teacher wellbeing:** Prioritising teacher wellbeing is essential for creating a positive school environment. A well-rounded approach includes offering professional development opportunities to support teachers' social and emotional needs so that teachers feel encouraged, valued and considered.
- **Better life outcomes:** A well-rounded education prepares students for success beyond the classroom. For example, schools might offer career exploration programs or financial literacy courses to equip students with practical life skills. Resilience and growth mindset activities empower students to overcome potential obstacles.
- **Community engagement:** Schools that prioritise a well-rounded approach to education are often known to have strong connections with their communities. Parent evenings that provide an extension to the students' learning and wellbeing activities help provide support and understanding to families in the school community.

Start with a wellbeing audit

Often the most frequent questions when it comes to implementing a whole-school approach is, 'Where do I start?' The answer is simple: start where you are! Schools often overlook the many successful programs and interventions already in operation. Therefore, the best first step is to conduct an audit of what is in place to establish a clear understanding of the current state of wellbeing and to identify opportunities for improvement.

In 'Leading Improvement in School Community Wellbeing' (2023), Emeritus Professor Donna Cross and Dr Leanne Lester provide guiding questions to help assess current wellbeing strengths and needs, determining required actions, and effectively implementing strategies for holistic improvement. The framework is structured around three key questions: 'What's happening?', 'What's working?' and 'What's next?'

For the audit, these three questions can be explored in relation to both staff and students.

Wellbeing audit for staff

Assessing the wellbeing of staff members is crucial for maintaining a healthy and productive workplace. It is challenging to say we take the wellbeing of our staff seriously if we do not understand where the staff are at with their interpretation of what is offered. Staff wellbeing encompasses various dimensions, including physical health, emotional support, job satisfaction, work-life balance and working towards alignment between personal values and beliefs with those of the school. Many schools have 'staff wellbeing' initiatives ('what's happening') but how often do we evaluate their effectiveness ('what's working')?

The benefits of conducting a staff wellbeing audit include:

- **Identifying stresses:** A wellbeing audit can highlight work-related stress that might impact staff members' physical and mental health.
- **Improving job satisfaction:** Understanding the needs and challenges faced by staff enables the implementation of changes that enhance job satisfaction, such as flexible work arrangements and professional development opportunities.
- **Fostering a positive workplace culture:** A supportive workplace culture that values staff wellbeing is important to the school's health. A wellbeing audit can help your school identify areas where culture can be improved to foster inclusivity, collaboration, connection, meaning and purpose.
- **Enhancing productivity:** By identifying and addressing wellbeing concerns, schools can improve staff productivity and engagement. Healthy work environments lead to better outcomes and higher productivity.
- **Supporting mental health initiatives:** A staff wellbeing audit can reveal areas where mental health support is needed and guide the implementation of targeted initiatives. These can be crucial in preventing burnout and feelings of disconnect, while enhancing employee engagement.
- **Revealing leadership strengths and areas for growth:** A staff wellbeing audit can provide leaders with an opportunity to gain authentic insights into their own strengths and areas for growth.

Conducting a staff wellbeing audit requires:

- **Planning and preparation:** Be sure to provide a clear definition of the audit's scope and your goals. Staff need to understand the purpose behind the audit. Identify the methods for data collection, such as surveys or focus groups, that will be most effective based on your context.
- **Data collection:** Gather data on staff wellbeing through surveys, interviews and observations. Include questions about work environment, job satisfaction and mental health resources that are both available and accessible.
- **Analysis and interpretation:** Analyse the data to identify areas for improvement and interpret findings in your own context.
- **Action planning:** Develop an action plan based on the information you have gathered, outlining specific strategies and timelines for improvement. Include opportunities to celebrate successes along the way.
- **Implementation:** Execute the plan and monitor its progress. Make necessary adjustments to ensure staff wellbeing initiatives are effective. Be sure to clearly articulate the staff benefits that underpin your plan.
- **Review and feedback:** Continuously evaluate the impact of the initiatives and get feedback from staff for ongoing improvement.

Wellbeing audit for students

A student wellbeing audit can examine various aspects including emotional health, social connections, academic pressures and access to support services. As with the staff audit, a student wellbeing audit provides opportunity to review current practices ('what's happening'), their effectiveness ('what's working') and plan for future strategies ('where to next').

The benefits of conducting a student wellbeing audit include:

- **Identifying academic stress:** A wellbeing audit can reveal sources of academic pressures for students, allowing schools or institutions to provide targeted support and resources to help overcome these pressures.
- **Improving student engagement:** Understanding the challenges students face can help educators create a more engaging and

supportive learning environment. Providing students with a voice in their learning and involving them in decision-making can improve engagement, academic performance and a sense of belonging.
- **Enhancing mental health support:** By identifying areas where mental health support is lacking for students, schools can implement more supportive approaches.
- **Fostering a sense of belonging:** A focus on student wellbeing can lead to a more inclusive environment where students feel valued and connected. Research identifies that creating a safe, supportive and inclusive environment where students of all backgrounds know they belong positively impacts students' emotional and social wellbeing.
- **Supporting overall academic success:** By addressing wellbeing concerns schools can improve students' academic performance and overall success. A holistic approach to student wellbeing can support young people's academic pursuits and personal development through habit development and goal-setting.
- **Demonstrating staff strengths and areas for growth:** Conducting a student wellbeing audit provides staff with insights into their strengths and areas for growth, which in turn enhances teacher effectiveness.

Conducting a student wellbeing audit requires:

- **Planning and preparation:** Define the audit's scope and goals, and choose appropriate methods for data collection, such as surveys or group discussions.
- **Data collection:** Collect data on student wellbeing through surveys, interviews and focus groups. Include questions about academic pressures, social interactions, things that cause worries and the access students have to support services.
- **Analysis and interpretation:** Analyse the data to identify patterns and areas for improvement. Interpret the findings within the context of your environment.
- **Action planning:** Develop an action plan based on your data analysis, outlining strategies and timelines for improving student wellbeing.
- **Implementation:** Execute the plan and monitor its progress. Adjust as necessary to ensure effective support for student wellbeing.
- **Review and feedback:** Continuously evaluate the impact of the initiatives and gather feedback from students for ongoing improvement. Student voice on what is working well is important.

Conducting a wellbeing audit for both staff and students is a proactive approach to enhance the overall health and wellbeing within any school environment. By identifying areas for improvement and implementing targeted strategies, schools can create supportive, inclusive and productive spaces for all community members. Prioritising this work demonstrates a commitment to the holistic wellbeing of everyone involved, fostering a positive culture that benefits all. Additionally, a wellbeing audit can reveal strengths and growth areas for leaders and staff members alike, helping to create a more cohesive and effective environment. This increases scope for everyone to flourish within the school context.

Following up with Appreciative Inquiry

Once you have conducted your audits you'll have a lot of information to digest. Knowing your aim is to further enhance the strengths of your programs, initiatives and interventions, your task is to now look at the areas requiring growth and move them forward. One such way is through Appreciative Inquiry.

David Cooperrider, alongside Suresh Srivastva, introduced the Appreciative Inquiry model in the 1980s as a deliberate move from traditional problem-solving approaches. Traditionally, organisations focused on 'fixing' problems. With an Appreciative Inquiry, the focus is on a strengths-based approach to generate positive ideas from which to grow, as opposed to working from a negative focus (deficit-based approach).

The Appreciative Inquiry model asks you to focus on the four Ds. After you have *defined* the topic, you are challenged to discover, dream, design and then deliver (see figure 2).

The questions used at the *discovery* stage help us identify what is good about current practice. They focus on the strengths of the human resources, physical resources or processes. These questions are framed in a positive manner, making us feel good while helping us think about opportunities for further growth and improvement.

The *dream* stage is about using our imagination to think of exciting new possibilities and goals for the future. Thought-provoking questions can be asked to engage with a variety of people in creative ways to spark meaningful conversations to lead towards progress and successful implementation. By asking these questions, we begin designing a roadmap for a successful future.

The *design* stage is a crucial phase where we brainstorm ways to turn our dream vision into a reality. It involves asking questions that guide us to think about the actions we need to implement to achieve our goals. We should reflect on past successes and identify specific steps for future projects at this stage.

In the *delivery* stage, we take the ideas from the design stage and find ways to make them happen. Decisions are made as to which ideas should be put into action, we then we plan how to make them happen and learn from the process.

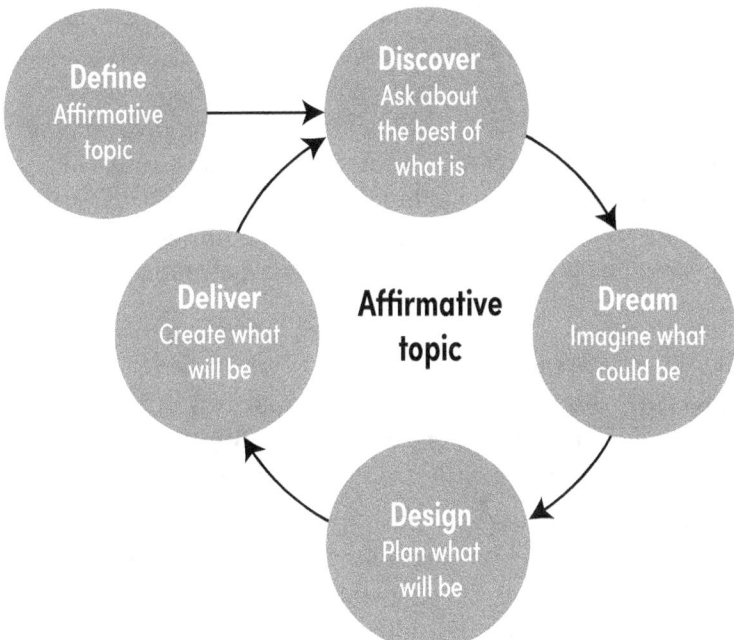

Figure 2: The Appreciative Inquiry model

For an Appreciative Inquiry to be successful, it must be based on these principles:

- **A positive focus:** At the heart of an Appreciative Inquiry is a positive mindset. Through his research, Cooperrider believed that focusing on strengths and successes helps inspire innovation and positive change.
- **Co-creation:** It is important to emphasise inclusive, collaborative processes when working towards school or organisational change to

help with everyone's alignment. This is based on Cooperrider's belief that a wider participation and input can lead to more meaningful, achievable and sustainable outcomes.
- **Appreciative eye:** Focusing on the current positives as well as the potential available within staff and the organisation helps us shift towards greater possibilities for the future.
- **Synchronicity:** When people start talking, asking questions, analysing possibilities and reflecting they begin to think about positive changes, which potentially creates a ripple effect throughout an organisation. Open dialogue helps combine inquiry and change as a merged process as opposed to being sequential.

The benefits of using an Appreciative Inquiry have been profound for developing a framework for whole-school wellbeing. I have witnessed first-hand the power as it transformed student conversations from problems to dreams of what could be. By embracing these practices and principles, schools can create environments were positivity, collaboration and continuous improvement thrive. Fostering a holistic approach, in which culture focuses on the strengths of the community, can lead to the following benefits:

- **Strengths-based culture:** By celebrating the strengths and achievements of staff, students and community members, Appreciative Inquiry helps cultivate a culture of positivity and empowerment in schools. This works to motivate people, increase morale and have a positive impact on everyone's wellbeing.
- **Collaborative problem-solving:** Appreciative Inquiry promotes collaborative problem-solving, where all stakeholders within the school community can come together to explore innovative solutions to challenges. Through this exploration, solutions can emerge naturally as people focus on what is working well and use these as a springboard on which to build.
- **Visionary leadership:** Through Appreciative Inquiry, school leaders can inspire a shared vision of a thriving, inclusive learning environment, where everyone works together with a shared purpose to achieve a common goal.
- **Sustainable change:** Unlike traditional change management approaches that may rely on external interventions, Appreciative Inquiry empowers schools to implement changes that are sustainable

from within. When you use Appreciative Inquiry to embed positive practices and mindsets into the fabric of the school culture, long-term adaptation and growth can be fostered.

Practical applications

There are many practical applications for an Appreciative Inquiry approach in schools. These can be utilised by staff and students alike to enhance school culture, teaching practices, student engagement, the physical environment and professional development or to address challenges such as poor behaviour and improving communication.

Some examples of practical applications include:

- **Staff meetings:** Incorporate Appreciative Inquiry principles into staff meetings so that staff have opportunities for reflection, problem-solving, collaboration and celebration.
- **Professional development:** When you design your professional development program around the strengths and expertise of your staff, you help create connection, improved performance and professional growth.
- **Student leadership summit:** Empower students to conduct an Appreciative Inquiry via a leadership summit. This helps foster a greater sense of agency, belonging and engagement within the school community. Students feel a greater sense of ownership knowing that their dreams for a brighter future at school are being valued.
- **Whole-school events:** When you examine what is currently offered, explore what the possibilities for additional offerings might be and then co-create a collective vision for future events. The community is more likely to embrace these ideas if they have a say in them. A recent example in my school was a Pyjama Day to raise awareness, understanding and donations for the Backpacks for SA Kids.

School readiness

I suggest using a self-assessment tool to discover how 'ready' your institution is to implement a wellbeing program or framework (see figure 3):

- **Define** the vision, objectives and outcomes behind the reason for the implementation.
- **Define** the 'readiness' of the community.

- **Define** the program, framework or initiative (identify current or future approaches):
    - Uncover your measurable long and short-term goals.
    - Set your goals, evaluate them and measure the outcome.
- **Decide** on what data will be required and how you will go about collecting it:
    - What will it look like for behaviours?
    - What will it look like for academics?
- **Design** the program and evaluation tools.
- **Define** and **design** what 'successful' implementation will look like:
    - Set your timelines and plan the scope and schedule for the data collection and analysis.

Figure 3: School readiness

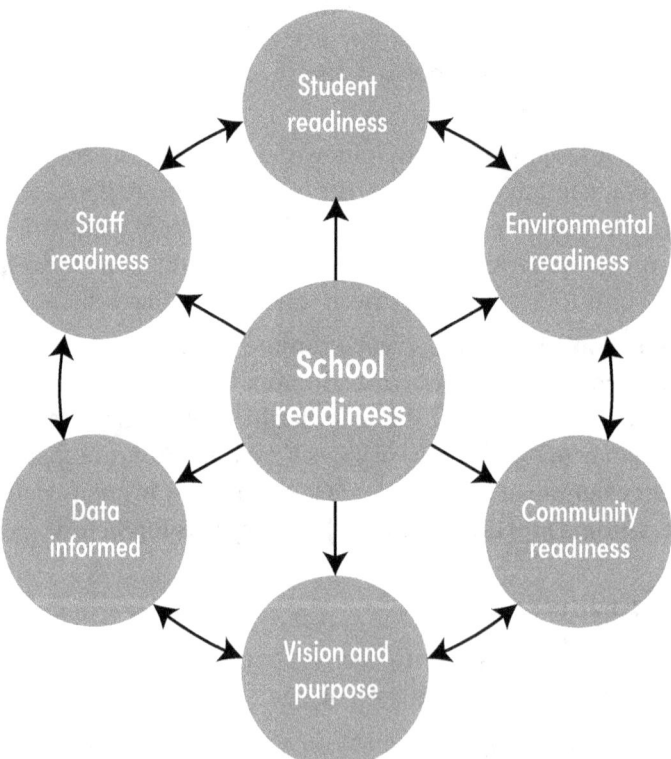

CHAPTER 6
IMPLEMENTING A WHOLE-SCHOOL APPROACH
Gratitude, Nature and Culture

Foster a whole-school approach, teach gratitude and nature's peace openly and subtly, and cultivate wellbeing.

The following quote above highlights the importance of fostering a school-wide wellbeing culture through strengths-based education:

> *Whole-school well-being approaches, such as those incorporating strengths-based education, aim to foster a school-wide culture where both students and staff thrive. Measurement and evaluation are crucial to ensure that well-being interventions lead to meaningful improvements in both the academic and personal development of students.*
>
> – White & Waters, 2015

The authors emphasise the need for measurement and evaluation to ensure the impact of the interventions you are planning. This naturally leads into a discussion of explicit and implicit teaching practices, both of which are essential in creating an environment where students and staff can thrive.

Explicit and implicit teaching

Wellbeing programs and initiatives can be incorporated into a whole-school approach in two ways. The first is through explicit teaching, where formal programs and curricula are used to teach wellbeing skills. The second is through implicit teaching, where wellbeing concepts are embedded into the school's culture and practices, allowing students to transfer and apply these skills to real-life contexts. When it comes to building student wellbeing, Professor Lea Waters (2021) summarises these approaches and explores benefits and downsides of both:

> *While explicit approaches (i.e., curriculums) build wellbeing through what we teach students, the implicit approach opens the door to enhancing wellbeing through how we teach (i.e., pedagogy).*

When wellbeing programs are taught explicitly in an educational setting, they are purposely designed to foster students' mental, emotional and physical health. To be most effective, these programs often integrate wellbeing topics into the daily curriculum, ensuring that concepts of self-care and emotional intelligence are woven into the fabric of everyday learning. For example, a typical day might start with a ten-minute mindfulness exercise, helping students centre themselves before academic activities begin. Teachers might lead discussions on various emotional regulation strategies, guiding students through identifying and managing feelings of anxiety, anger or sadness. Activities could include journalling exercises to reflect on personal experiences, role-playing scenarios to practise conflict resolution, and group projects that emphasise teamwork and effective communication. Physical health can be addressed through structured physical education classes that promote regular exercise, healthy eating habits and overall fitness. By providing these tools and experiences, the whole-school program aims to build resilient and well-rounded students capable of navigating the complexities of life.

Explicitly teaching wellbeing enables schools to:

- Develop a scope and sequence to ensure that all desired aspects are covered through topics such as being your best self, emotional regulation, mindfulness, coping strategies and healthy relationships.
- Utilise curricula that are designed by experts in their fields and, therefore, have quality resources which enable the implementation of evidence-based programs targeting specific aspects of wellbeing, such as skills in resiliency or respectful relationships.
- Ensure age-appropriateness of the learning.
- Contextualise and target skills, such as communication, empathy, inclusive language, staying safe online and conflict resolution.

When you incorporate explicit wellbeing teaching within the school context, it is then woven implicitly through school life and contributes to establishing and maintaining a supportive, respectful and inclusive school culture.

Reflection: Explicit wellbeing teaching

- How will the selected curriculum align with our school's definition of wellbeing?
- Does the curriculum align to our context?
- Does the curriculum align to our wellbeing framework?
- Is the curriculum scientifically informed and evidence-based?
- Is the curriculum agile and adaptable?

Examples of wellbeing curriculum

- Bounce Back!
- Friendology
- Zones of Regulation
- Grow Your Mind
- Resilience Project
- Growing with Gratitude
- Personal Well-Being Lessons for Secondary Schools
- Healthy Minds

These can be supported with a tailor-made series of incursions:

- Respectful relationships
- Nature education
- Day of Hope
- The benefits of sleep
- Cybersafety – staying safe online
- Violence prevention program

You can also organise parent information sessions on topics such as:

- Cybersafety
- Resilience education
- Transitioning smoothly between school sections.

The benefits of explicitly teaching wellbeing skills and concepts include:

- **Improved understanding of character strengths:**
  - Being able to see strengths in self and others.
  - Finding ways to boost strengths.
  - Being able to identify when our strengths may work against us.

- **Enhanced emotional intelligence:**
  - Recognising and understanding your own and others' emotions.
  - Improved skills in emotional regulation.
  - Developing a greater sense of empathy.
  - Improved relationships across the whole school.
  - Creating a more supportive and harmonious school environment.

- **Improved coping strategies:**
    - Having practical tools for dealing with challenging situations and setbacks.
    - Improved resilience.
    - A growth mindset.
    - Being better prepared to handle the pressures of academics, social dynamics or personal issues.
- **A more positive impact on accomplishment:**
    - Enhanced concentration and motivation.
    - Use of techniques such as mindfulness, goal setting and time management to improve academic outcomes.
    - Increased focus and organisation.
- **Improved relationships:**
    - A more inclusive and positive culture, with reduced 'mean on purpose' behaviours.
    - A more cohesive and supportive environment that develops positive classroom dynamics and enhances learning.

While explicitly teaching a wellbeing curriculum will enhance student wellbeing, it cannot be the only factor in achieving a whole-school approach or expected to lead to cultural change unless it is supported in other ways.

Implicit teaching of wellbeing in schools is a way to subtly integrate wellbeing into the overall school culture and daily routines, making social, emotional, psychological and physical health an authentic component of the learning environment. This helps to create a supportive, encouraging and engaging culture through everyday interactions and practices. We know that students learn from teachers' modelling. When teachers model positive behaviours and emotional regulation, demonstrating how they cope with stress or disappointment constructively, students become more likely to mirror those behaviours. Examples such as taking deep breaths, discussing feelings openly and using problem-solving techniques during conflicts all work to reinforce the skills we are teaching through our explicit programs.

When wellbeing is woven into the fabric of the school, classroom activities are structured to encourage cooperation and mutual respect, collaboration and a sense of belonging. Additionally, inclusive language and positive reinforcement are used to create a safe and welcoming environment for all students, helping them find meaning and connection in their learning environment.

The design of physical spaces also plays a crucial role. Classrooms can be arranged to reduce stress and promote comfort, incorporating elements such as natural light, quiet zones for relaxation, comfortable seating, and displays of inspirational messages and student artwork. By embedding these subtle, yet impactful, practices into daily routines, wellbeing becomes an intrinsic part of the students' experience, encouraging them to thrive academically and personally.

Outside of the classroom, practices that promote the desired culture of the school add to the whole-school approach to wellbeing. Schools can implement policies that promote a positive environment by fostering positive relationships and helping students engage in their learning. These policies can also support students in finding meaning and purpose in their role within the school, experiencing a sense of accomplishment, and developing positive emotions (PERMA).

By weaving these practices into the fabric of the school day, wellbeing is promoted implicitly, creating an environment where students naturally develop resilience, empathy and move towards a more flourishing life.

Reflection: Implicit wellbeing teaching

- What are the behaviours we want our students to display?
- What authentic ways can we bring the skills taught in wellbeing lessons into our daily practices and routines across the school?
- What skills do we want our students to take into their lives beyond school?
- What part will staff and student agency play in developing our plans?
- What policies need to be developed to prioritise wellbeing and support student and staff mental health?
- What areas in our school either promote or restrict wellbeing?

Examples of ways to implicitly weave wellbeing practices into the school day

- Begin each day with a mood check-in. Ask students to identify which 'zone' they are in and what they need to do to be best prepared for learning.
- Ask students to set a goal that is achievable over a short period of time to work towards. Have them unpack what obstacles may stand in their way and develop a plan to counter them.
- Ask students to maintain a gratitude diary to record things that went well for them each day before leaving school.
- Build a wellbeing culture into your assemblies to highlight authentic connections that students have made with wellbeing concepts – displaying character strengths and so on.
- Create a 'Better Buddy' system within your school context between different age groups to build a community of care and mutual respect.
- Develop a co-curricular program that offers a range of opportunities for students to develop a sense of belonging to the wider school community.
- Create a staff meeting culture that recognises staff, celebrates their achievements and acknowledges their human (non-employee) side.

The benefits of implicitly weaving wellbeing skills, concepts and practices include:

- A natural connection to real-world situations:
    - Wellbeing practices become habitual and part of the normal school routine and culture.
    - Students are provided opportunities to create real-world connections with wellbeing scenarios and problems to solve.
- Enhanced social and emotional skills:
    - Students develop a sense of empathy. They learn cooperative skills and become more adept at conflict resolution.
    - Students develop greater understanding and awareness of their emotions and what it means to pay attention to how they are feeling.

- Students feel more comfortable discussing emotions and seeking support.
- A greater range of coping strategies:
  - Students develop more control and regulation around their emotions.
  - Students become more confident to seek support.
  - Students can learn to see setbacks as a natural part of life.
  - Students develop a more comprehensive toolkit to emotionally deal with a range of situations.

Explicit and implicit methods complement each other by addressing different aspects of wellbeing. Explicit programs focus on skill acquisition and intervention and developing foundational knowledge, while implicit approaches emphasise cultural norms, relational dynamics and community support, reinforcing these concepts through daily practices and interactions.

Together, these approaches create a comprehensive and balanced approach to supporting staff and student wellbeing. They contribute to a whole-school approach to wellbeing, where educators, students, and families collaborate to create an environment that prioritises mental health, resilience and emotional intelligence as essential components of education and personal development. When we combine the explicit and implicit approaches to wellbeing, we create incredible opportunities for staff and students to develop the skills they need for a flourishing life, as shown in table 9.

Table 9: Explicit and implicit methods of teaching wellbeing

	Explicit	Implicit
Wellbeing skill development	Structured lessons and activities that focus on specific skills.	Students learn to apply these skills in real-life situations within the school environment.
Consistent reinforcement of concepts	Establishes a foundational understanding.	Reinforces these principles through consistent integration into daily routine.

	Explicit	Implicit
Positive school environment	*Both approaches contribute to creating a supportive and inclusive school atmosphere where wellbeing is valued.*	
	Teaches students the necessary skills.	Reinforces these values through everyday interactions.
Personalised and contextual learning	Provide targeted interventions, based on the needs of the school/students.	Create an environment where all students feel supported and encouraged.

A whole-school approach to wellbeing that integrates explicit wellbeing lessons into the curriculum and fosters a school culture that supports wellbeing through all interactions and policies aims to meet the needs of the whole child across all aspects of school life. This leads to enhanced learning outcomes and overall long-term wellbeing for everyone. These schools provide opportunities for students to not only learn about wellbeing concepts, but to internalise their practice to utilise the skills more effectively. This holistic approach not only benefits individual students and staff but also contributes to a more cohesive and positive school community.

Table 10 gives examples of how three specific wellbeing initiatives can be taught explicitly and implicitly.

Table 10: Explicit and implicit teaching of wellbeing initiatives

Example: Zones of Regulation	
Explicitly teach:	**So they can be implicitly woven into:**
Each of the zones and the emotions they represent	Students' understanding and awareness of their emotional state at various times throughout the day
Identifying triggers that spark emotional reactions	Strategies to deal with these emotions as they arise
Positive decision making and problem solving	Making appropriate choices form those available

Example: Friendology	
Explicitly teach:	**So they can be implicitly woven into:**
The four Friendship Facts	Students' understanding that throughout their school day/life, their friendships will change and that is okay
Friendship Fires and Mean on Purpose behaviours	Students' interactions with their peers in the yard and classroom
Example: Bounce Back!	
Explicitly teach:	**So they can be implicitly woven into:**
Catastrophising exacerbates your worries	Students' ability to unpack a situation to determine realistic versus catastrophic thinking
Life has ups and downs but you can bounce back	Students' thinking patterns and the key messages for them to tell themselves

Cultivating an attitude of gratitude

Practising gratitude every day has amazing benefits that touch every part of our lives. Gratitude makes us feel better both mentally and physically. When we get into the habit of noticing and appreciating the good things in our daily lives, it helps us stay strong and more emotionally balanced.

Research shows that gratitude lowers stress, reduces anxiety and lifts our spirits, shifting our focus from what we are missing to what we have. It helps build a sense of happiness even when things seem challenging. The flow-on effect is that our relationships are strengthened, because expressing gratitude deepens our connections with family, friends and the people we work with. It builds deeper trust and understanding.

In addition to boosting our mental health, studies suggest that the practice of daily gratitude has benefits for our physical wellbeing. It is believed that grateful people tend to have lower blood pressure, a stronger immune system and better sleep patterns. Having a strong sense of gratitude eases stress on our bodies which supports a healthier heart and our overall physical resilience.

The University of California conducted a study on patients with heart failure. They found: 'It seems that a more grateful heart is indeed a more healthy heart, and that gratitude journalling is an easy way to support cardiac health' (Mills et al. 2015).

Making gratitude a part of our daily routine not only enriches our own lives but also creates a kinder and more supportive community. It encourages us to notice and appreciate the kindness of others, fostering a culture of compassion and empathy that helps everyone thrive. When we embrace gratitude every day, we're setting ourselves and those around us up for a happier and more resilient journey through life.

In his book *Growing with Gratitude* (2022), Ash Manuel highlights the profound ways that gratitude can be used as a transformative practice. Manuel explores the expansive benefits of integrating gratitude into our routines of daily life. In a school setting, these could include:

- **Cultivating positive emotions:**
  - Gratitude directs our attention to the positive aspects of life, and fosters feelings of happiness and contentment. Research suggests that regularly expressing gratitude can elevate our mood and increase our levels of positive emotions.

- **Building mental and emotional resilience:**
  - Gratitude builds resilience by encouraging a positive outlook on adversity. Studies indicate lower levels of stress and anxiety amongst individuals who practise gratitude.
  - Being grateful teaches us to find the silver lining in challenging situations, fostering emotional strength and adaptive coping skills.

- **Building connections:**
  - Gratitude is a powerful tool for strengthening relationships and fostering a sense of belonging.
  - Habits of gratitude promote kindness and empathy among peers, where the expression of appreciation for each other can be shared.
  - Gratitude enhances social bonds by increasing trust and promoting prosocial behaviours.
  - Gratitude creates supportive environments in which everyone feels valued and understood.

- **Enhancing physical and mental wellbeing:**
    - Practising gratitude boosts self-esteem by drawing our attention to personal achievements and strengths.
    - Practising gratitude encourages us to savour positive experiences and remain present in the moment, enhancing our physiological health and resilience against illness.
- **Empowering personal growth and self-esteem:**
    - When individuals acknowledge their own contributions through personal gratitude reflections it helps reinforce a positive self-image.
    - A mindset of self-appreciation enables individuals who practise gratitude to experience greater self-worth. They are therefore more likely to engage in goal-directed behaviours.

Examples of practising gratitude

- Keep a daily gratitude journal. To develop a deeper experience, make sure you record the 'why' of your gratitude.
- Share expressions of love and appreciation with people in your life. Randomly select a different person each day to let them know how much you value and appreciate them.
- When you're walking, stop, look and admire something beautiful in nature. Remind yourself of the wonders of our natural environment.
- Smile regularly. Remember that smiling is contagious. When you smile at someone, they will likely smile back. You will both receive a rush of dopamine.
- Place messages around your home, car, office and classroom to remind you of everything you have to be grateful. Focus on the things that you may otherwise take for granted.
- Practise self-gratitude. Each week, record something you are able to do for which you are grateful.
- Use regular 'shout-outs'. Develop a practice of recognising people publicly, such as at staff meetings, for who they are and what they contribute.

Wellbeing and the natural environment

Our environment plays a crucial role in enhancing our wellbeing. Whether it is through incorporating natural elements such as plants, sunlight and fresh air into our learning and working spaces, or by creating organised and clutter-free areas to enhance focus and productivity, we can reduce stress and improve both our and our students' mood. Additionally, using natural colours, tones and comfortable furniture can create a sense of calm and belonging. By intentionally designing our surroundings to support wellbeing we can significantly boost the overall mental and physical health of all school members.

The benefits of nature play have been well documented for some time. These multisensory experiences, where students explore different textures, smells and sounds, have been proven to have significant benefits to their physical, cognitive, social and emotional development. Moving beyond the structured play of playgrounds helps evoke an awakening of imagination as they experience open-ended play using natural materials. This type of play encourages creativity and problem-solving skills, as children interact with their environment in unstructured ways.

Research over the past few years has shown a significant increase in the amount of screen time in which young children are engaged. This rise in screen time is linked to a sedentary lifestyle and can have negative impacts on a child's health and development. Opening the doors and encouraging children to play outside in nature helps steer them away from the use of technology and into a less structured environment. Being outdoors promotes physical activity and exposes children to the natural elements, which can enhance their sensory experiences and appreciation for the environment.

The busyness of life means that for many children, their activities are incredibly structured – sporting, musical, academic. They have routines and plans timetabled to accommodate their varied interests. While structured activities have their benefits, it is crucial to balance them with unstructured playtime in natural settings. This balance allows children to decompress, reduce stress and develop a sense of freedom and autonomy.

As a school, it is important to provide experiences in which children can engage with the natural world which, in turn, will provide benefits to their wellbeing. Simple observations of children playing in nature clearly identify character strengths at work through resilience, cooperation and adaptability. Nature play helps children develop social skills as they interact with peers in a natural setting, negotiate roles and solve conflicts. It also fosters a connection to the environment, instilling a sense of stewardship and responsibility towards nature. By prioritising nature play, schools can support children's holistic development, nurturing their physical, emotional and cognitive growth while developing character strengths.

Some of the benefits of time spent in nature include:

- **Increased levels of creativity and freedom for self-expression:**
    - Solving problems – making connections to the world around them and then applying their knowledge to similar situations.
    - Creating adventures.

- **An appreciation of the beauty of the natural environment:**
    - Spending time exploring through the senses.

- **Promotion of curiosity through exploration and discovery:**
    - Natural wonder.
    - Risk-taking.

- **Improved self-regulation:**
    - Managing emotions in difficult situations.
    - Recognising, processing and responding to feelings.
    - Learning to be flexible.

- **Increased levels of kindness through working together:**
    - Sharing resources.
    - Understanding other perspectives and ideas.

The result of this can be a significant increase in children's resilience as they learn to negotiate various risk factors. Being actively engaged in these decisions helps children develop an increased ability to become better risk assessors as they learn to navigate their environment. This process of risk negotiation is crucial for their development; it builds confidence and self-reliance. Without predefined instructions, such as how to make a mud pie or build a tree cubby, children are encouraged to take risks and solve their own problems.

This kind of play fosters critical thinking and creativity, as children must come up with their own solutions and strategies. It also enhances their ability to work collaboratively with peers, as they often need to communicate and cooperate to achieve their goals. Moreover, engaging in nature play helps children understand the consequences of their actions in a safe and controlled manner, thereby improving their decision-making skills.

By facing and overcoming challenges in their natural play environment, children learn to cope with failures and setbacks, which is an essential part of building resilience. This resilience extends beyond play and can positively impact their academic performance and social interactions. Encouraging nature play, therefore, not only supports children's immediate enjoyment and development but also equips them with the skills necessary for their future wellbeing and success.

Children love being able to explore through nature play. Here's what some children have told me:

- 'Nature play is awesome fun. I like to build things with sticks. I hear children talking about how to do things. I see children having fun and excitement. I feel happy and calm.' (Age six)
- 'I like looking after the area. I like making things with the sticks and stones. When I am playing in the nature play area I feel green [in the green zone of regulation] and calm. I like to hear nature. I see children playing nicely and others that are arguing then solving their problems calmly.' (Age seven)
- 'Nature play looks shady and calm. You can hear the sounds of kids rustling through the leaves as they run across the nature. You can hear the rainbow birds chirping as they fly to their nests. You can feel the cool breezy air as you run past the trees and the huts that people have made. You can feel the cold dirt rushing through your fingers as you play. You can see all the kids playing and creating shops with sticks, leaves, water and sand. I love nature play because it feels relaxing and calming.' (Age ten)

Example of a student-led nature play initiative

Trinity College North collaborated with Nature Play SA to conduct a series of experiential sessions with student leaders. The intended outcome was to develop a concept for a wellbeing garden that is welcoming and stimulating for students. The project supported student agency and inclusivity, fostering a deeper connection between students and the natural environment and supporting mental and emotional wellbeing.

The aim for the project was to have a positive impact on the school community and help create a lasting and welcoming space for students to enjoy. The project also offered numerous educational opportunities for students to learn about wellbeing in nature, local biodiversity, sustainability and design.

Table 11 shows how the project unfolded.

Table 11: Student-led wellbeing garden project

Planning	
Student Workshop 1	Student leaders workshop: • Setting the framework for co-design, observing on-site, understanding the benefits of nature and auditing natural assets. • Additional consideration: Engage a Kaurna (local First Nations) leader to work with students from the outset of the project.
Student Workshop 2	Student-led hands-on ideation process: • Facilitated ideation session to brainstorm ideas for the garden elements (wayfinding, seating, fixed and loose parts, sensory areas) and sustainability/maintenance concepts. • Learners establish design principles for the garden. • Mosaic of ideas to feed back to the school community for further consultation. • Additional consideration – engage Kaurna leader and a landscape architect.
Student Workshop 3	Student-led design process: • Learners use top-view map resource to create a mud map of the design elements to be included in the garden.
Final presentation of designs and submission for costing	

Not all schools are lucky enough to have beautiful and natural environments in which their students can play – for example, inner-city schools may have limited outdoor spaces. If this is the case, there are still ways to make your school environment work for you to enhance wellbeing.

As humans, we all have a little voice inside our head that sends signals to us when we are in different environments. All schools have areas that students either feel great to be in or feel oppressed by and experience low levels of energy. A simple task to do is ask the staff and students for feedback about these areas. A simple question like 'Which areas in our school do you feel happy to be in?' can lead to great conversations around areas that either promote or detract from a sense of wellbeing. These can then initiate agency around the redevelopment of the spaces to become more wellbeing focused.

One simple, practical way to use what we have in a school environment is to follow the '5, 4, 3, 2, 1' grounding exercise. This helps us manage stress and reduce anxiety by focusing on the present moment. This technique uses your five senses and helps shift attention away from unhelpful thoughts to a focus on your surroundings. The effectiveness of this method comes from engaging multiple senses, requiring focus on your present environment. These thoughts help promote a calming of our nervous system and in turn reduce our negative or unhelpful thinking.

Activity: 5, 4, 3, 2, 1 grounding

This is an example that can be used, but an alternative is to work with staff and/or students to create their own and personalise it (e.g. drill down into the specifics of their learning/working environments).

Responses should be fairly quick and immediate to shift thinking.

- What are five things that you see around you? (e.g. pencil, tree.)
- What are four things around you that you can safely touch? (e.g. hair, lawn, blanket.)
- What are three things you can hear? (e.g. birds, children laughing.)
- What are two things you can smell? (e.g. a scent in the air, the smell of soap on your hands.)
- What is one thing you can taste? (e.g. your hot chocolate, your sandwich.)

CHAPTER 7

UNSTOPPABLE GROWTH

Building Resilience, Grit and Student Agency

Unlock the power within. Build resilience, master social and emotional skills, and foster grit and student agency for unstoppable growth and success.

The ability to develop flourishing students has become central to the role of any educational institution. This involves teaching our young people the key skills of resilience, understanding emotions, perseverance and self-regulation. Resilience can be developed when students feel supported. By helping students understand and manage their emotions through social-emotional learning (SEL), we equip them with the tools they need to face difficulties and grow stronger. Perseverance and grit, which keep students working towards their goals even when things get tough, are essential and currently appear lacking as prominent traits in our students. Encouraging a growth mindset enables students to learn to see challenges as opportunities for improvement.

A major component of empowering students is helping them develop self-regulation, which allows them to manage their learning and emotions effectively. When these skills are combined and emphasised, students are better prepared to handle stress, make good decisions, and take control of their learning. By putting students at the centre of these efforts, they become more confident and resilient, ready to achieve their goals and face life's challenges.

Building resilience in our young people

In chapter 1 we looked at how to build resilience in adults. But what about our students? The current state of resilience in our young people reflects both challenges and opportunities for educators. The response to the Covid-19 global crisis showed that many young individuals are able to demonstrate adaptability and resourcefulness. We also understand that today's youth are the most likely to react proactively to social injustices, environmental issues and ensuring a sense of inclusivity for all. They use technology for education and to maintain social connection, displaying innovation and resilience. However, they also face issues of mental ill-health, including anxiety and depression, that can be exacerbated by their constant exposure to the digital world and to societal pressures. This demonstrates the need for resilience-building programs in schools to provide the necessary tools and support for young people to thrive through challenges and adversity.

Developing resilience in students offers numerous benefits that extend beyond the classroom. Resilient students are better equipped to handle stress, adapt to change and overcome challenges, leading to improved academic performance and emotional wellbeing. They develop a positive outlook and problem-solving skills which enhance their ability to navigate social relationships and conflicts. Furthermore, resilience fosters a sense of self-efficacy and confidence, enabling students to pursue their goals and persevere when faced with challenges. Ultimately, cultivating resilience prepares students for the complexities of life, promoting lifelong success and personal growth.

In earlier chapters we explored what resilience is and isn't. How we define resilience as a school impacts what we expect from our students. Knowing that we can develop and improve our own levels of resilience should become a greater driver in our intent to deliver intentional opportunities for our students to become more resilient. Again, explicitly teaching the skills and then implicitly weaving them authentically through the school provides greater depth of understanding and ability to transfer from theory to practice (see table 12).

Table 12: How to build resilience in students

Build on strengths	• Deliver activities for students to recognise their strengths.
	• Make character strengths a focus to enhance the best of who students are.
	• Make 'what went well' a focus in the classroom to draw attention to the positive aspects of school.
Ensure students feel connected	• Deliver team-building activities to develop and nurture trust among students.
	• Have students complete a sociogram of friends so you can understand who does not appear to have a connection within the class/year level. This provides opportunities for you to create experiences to change this.
	• Conduct the Hand of Trust activity, where students name five people in their lives they trust to keep them safe. For older students, delve deeper by having them explain why the specific names appear.

Explicitly teach coping strategies	Demonstrate specific problem-solving strategies: <ul><li>Define the problem – brainstorm possible outcomes – look at best-case and worst-case scenarios.</li><li>Cultivate mental agility to view situations from multiple perspectives and think flexibly.</li><li>Conduct role-playing where students take on different characters or viewpoints in a scenario, exploring how different individuals might perceive the same situation.</li><li>Organise debates where students argue for a position opposite to their initial belief.</li><li>Provide brain teasers and puzzles requiring students to think outside the box and explore multiple solutions.</li><li>Find time for mindfulness activities, allowing the brain to slow.</li></ul>
Encourage self-awareness	<ul><li>Help students develop self-awareness by prompting them to pay attention to their thoughts and emotions at various times throughout the day.</li><li>Make nature walks/outdoor time where focus is given to thoughts and feelings part of your class's daily routine.</li></ul>
Cultivate optimistic thinking	<ul><li>Work with students to unpack what helpful and unhelpful thinking looks like, sounds like and feels like.</li><li>Encourage them to maintain gratitude journals to record what is going well.</li><li>Help them explore what is in or out of their control.</li><li>Explore what catastrophising is and how is it unhelpful.</li><li>Set goals and celebrate successes.</li><li>Support them to learn to overcome any obstacles.</li><li>Encourage them to find and record something that gave meaning and purpose to their day.</li></ul>

Building social and emotional capacity

We all know that children's social and emotional health has a significant impact on their development and learning. Research clearly shows that children with higher levels of wellbeing are generally happier, more motivated to learn and perform better academically. In contrast, we know those with social and emotional challenges often struggle to follow directions, participate in activities, and may experience a loss of connection, lower self-esteem and academic difficulties. Therefore, the social and emotional health of our young people is a crucial component of a child's development and potential for a fulfilling life.

Within our institutions, we can support this aspect of wellbeing by creating environments that encourage social interactions and by building trusting relationships and engaging in intentional teaching. For the main part, most of what I am about to share simply constitutes good teaching practice.

Creating a safe and supportive environment

A classroom environment that feels safe and supportive is foundational for social-emotional learning (SEL). This involves establishing clear and consistent rules that promote respect and empathy is crucial. By building trusting and positive relationships between students, as well as between students and teachers, we can foster a strong sense of community. Encouraging open communication is essential; it creates opportunities for students to express their thoughts and feelings without fear of judgement, which contributes to a supportive and inclusive learning environment.

Integrating SEL into the curriculum

Incorporating SEL authentically into lessons and activities makes it a natural part of the learning process. You can do this via:

- **Literature and stories:** Selecting books and stories that highlight social and emotional themes. Discussing characters' emotions, decisions and relationships.
- **Role-playing and simulations:** Engaging students in role-playing activities to practise and develop the skills of empathy, conflict resolution and collaborative problem-solving.
- **Reflective writing:** Encouraging students to write about their experiences, emotions and relationships in journals or reflective narratives.

Explicitly teaching SEL skills

Dedicate time to explicitly teach SEL skills through direct instruction and opportunities for practice. This can include teaching self-awareness to enable students to recognise and name their emotions and provide strategies for managing them, such as deep breathing or positive self-talk. Empathy-building can be fostered by engaging students in activities that promote learning to see different perspectives and understanding others' feelings. Additionally, conflict resolution skills can be taught and practised by using techniques such as 'I' statements and finding win-win solutions.

Role-modelling SEL skills

Teachers and school staff play a crucial part in role-modelling SEL skills for students. By consistently demonstrating healthy emotional regulation, educators show students how to manage their own emotions effectively, even in challenging situations. Through the use of clear and effective communication, teachers not only convey their own thoughts and feelings in a respectful manner but encourage students to do the same. By showcasing empathetic behaviour in interactions with students and their colleagues, teachers create a classroom environment that fosters mutual respect and understanding, helping students learn to appreciate different perspectives and develop their own empathy skills.

Key resource

The Resilience and Wellbeing Toolbox: Building Character and Competence through Life's Ups and Downs (Nawana Parker, 2020) is a practical guide to fostering resilience and wellbeing in students as they develop skills such as emotional regulation, empathy, persistence, problem-solving, optimism and gratitude. It provides guidance on SEL frameworks, research-based strategies and a flexible implementation framework.

Encourage peer collaboration and support

Promote a classroom culture where students support each other's social and emotional growth using the following strategies:

- **Peer mentoring:** Pair older or more experienced students with younger peers for mentorship and guidance.

- **Collaborative projects:** Design group activities that require cooperation, communication and collective problem-solving.
- **Circle time and group discussions:** Regularly engage students in group discussions where they can share their thoughts and feelings and practise active listening.

Assessing social and emotional growth

Monitoring and assessing students' social and emotional development is essential for providing targeted support and celebrating their progress. This can be achieved by using various assessment methods, such as regularly observing students' interactions and behaviours in different settings to capture a holistic view of their social skills. Self-assessments also play a crucial role by encouraging students to reflect on their personal growth and identify areas for improvement through tools and surveys. In addition to these methods, gathering feedback from peers and teachers is invaluable as it provides diverse perspectives and insights, offering a well-rounded understanding of each student's social and emotional skills.

Developing grit and perseverance

The qualities of grit and perseverance, which we touched on in chapter 1, can profoundly impact student wellbeing. It's therefore important for educators to find ways to develop these traits in our students.

Psychologist Angela Duckworth (2017) popularised the term 'grit' to describe having both passion and perseverance towards achieving our long-term goals. Grit is our ability to sustain the deep-seated commitment, effort and resilience required to overcome obstacles and persist through challenges we face. Perseverance, a closely related concept, involves maintaining our course of action despite any difficulties or barriers that threaten successful achievement.

Research has consistently shown that grit and perseverance are critical predictors of our ability to be successful across the many facets in our lives. According to Duckworth, individuals with high levels of grit are more likely to achieve their long-term goals because they are willing to endure hardship and maintain their efforts over time.

Our wellbeing is built from the physical, emotional, psychological and social dimensions of our lives, and grit and perseverance can significantly enhance these in several ways. These include:

- **Emotional resilience:** Students who cultivate grit and perseverance are better equipped to handle stress and setbacks. They tend to have a more positive outlook on challenges, viewing them as opportunities for growth rather than insurmountable obstacles. This mindset contributes to improved emotional resilience, which is a critical aspect of overall wellbeing.
- **Academic achievement:** Perseverance and grit are strongly correlated with academic success. Students who demonstrate these traits are more likely to persist through difficult coursework, seek help when needed and remain committed to their educational goals. This persistence not only leads to higher academic performance but also boosts students' self-confidence and sense of accomplishment.
- **Social relationships:** The development of grit and perseverance can positively impact students' social interactions. Students who persevere through social challenges and conflicts are more likely to build stronger, more supportive relationships. This can lead to a greater sense of belonging and connectedness within the school community.
- **Goal-setting and motivation:** Students with high levels of grit are more adept at setting and pursuing long-term goals. They are motivated by their passions and are willing to invest time and effort into achieving their aspirations. This intrinsic motivation enhances their engagement in school activities and fosters a sense of purpose and direction.

Caroline Adams Miller, a prominent researcher in positive psychology, has made significant contributions to our understanding of grit and perseverance. Miller's work highlights the importance of mindset and goal-setting in developing these traits. In her book *Getting Grit: The Evidence-Based Approach to Cultivating Passion, Perseverance, and Purpose* (2017) Miller emphasises that individuals who set meaningful, challenging goals and approach them with determination are more likely to develop grit. Miller also explores the role of self-efficacy in cultivating perseverance. Her findings suggest that students who believe in their ability to overcome challenges are more resilient and persistent. This belief in oneself, coupled with effective goal-setting strategies, can enhance students' capacity to navigate difficulties and achieve their objectives.

Practical strategies for developing students' grit include:

- **Encourage a growth mindset:** Promote the belief that abilities and intelligence can be developed through effort and perseverance. Encourage students to view challenges as opportunities for growth rather than as threats to their competence.
- **Set realistic but challenging goals:** Help students set specific, achievable goals that are aligned with their interests and passions. Provide support and guidance as they work towards these goals and celebrate their progress and achievements.
- **Model perseverance:** Demonstrate grit and perseverance in your own work and interactions with students by consistently showing dedication and resilience. Share personal stories of overcoming challenges, including the specific strategies and techniques you used to persevere, to inspire and motivate students. This helps students see the value of persistence and provides them with real-life examples of how to handle difficulties.
- **Foster a supportive environment:** Establish an environment where perseverance and hard work are celebrated and students feel safe taking risks. Provide constructive feedback that highlights strengths and areas for improvement, and encourage students to view mistakes and setbacks as learning opportunities. This approach fosters a growth mindset and supports continuous improvement.
- **Teach coping strategies:** Provide students with various tools and techniques to manage stress and overcome obstacles. These strategies include mindfulness practices to help students stay present and reduce anxiety, along with time management skills to prioritise tasks and use time efficiently. Additionally, problem-solving strategies empower students to identify issues, brainstorm solutions and implement effective action plans.

Self-regulation as a skill and a strength

Self-regulation is a multifaceted concept that plays a crucial role in the development of both learning and wellbeing. It's a term we have seen take greater prominence in education. Self-regulation empowers individuals to manage their emotions, thoughts and behaviours to achieve personal and academic goals, ultimately contributing to their academic, psychological, emotional, physical and social health. As a character strength, self-regulation involves managing emotions, impulses and behaviours in a way that reflects your own beliefs and principles while also respecting societal rules and expectations. This capacity for emotional and behavioural control helps individuals manage anger, frustration and stress while resisting temptations and impulsive actions. Its broad application extends across the many interactions we have through personal relationships, professional settings, online activities and social interactions, significantly enhancing an individual's emotional wellbeing and decision-making abilities. Self-regulation, which develops through personal growth and regular practice, is crucial for thriving in many aspects of our lives. When we work on controlling our emotions, impulses and actions, we become more resilient and better equipped to handle any stress or challenge we may face. Self-regulation also helps build stronger and more meaningful relationships by improving communication, empathy and understanding and can lead to better wellbeing by feeling more balanced and fulfilled.

Self-regulated learning has a specific focus on managing cognitive and metacognitive processes to enhance learning outcomes and academic performance. This involves taking control of the learning process by setting clear, achievable goals, monitoring progress, employing effective learning strategies such as time management, organisation and reflective practices, and assessing the effectiveness of these strategies. Our primary goal in developing self-regulated learners is to improve students' academic performance and foster independent, adaptive learning, while also supporting their wellbeing by reducing stress levels and anxious thoughts associated with academic pressures. By promoting a sense of control and mastery over their learning, self-regulation contributes to students' confidence and emotional health. Shyam Barr, an educational researcher and lecturer, focuses on self-regulated learning in his book *Educate to Self-Regulate* (2024). Barr explores how students can actively manage their learning by setting goals, monitoring progress and reflecting on outcomes. Barr highlights the critical role of educators in fostering environments that encourage student autonomy and self-direction. He advocates integrating technology, such as digital tools and platforms, to support self-regulated learning and stresses the importance of effective assessment and feedback. His research offers practical strategies for teachers, including goal-setting, strategy instruction and technology use to enhance self-regulated learning skills.

Barr's work on self-regulated learning is also closely linked to self-regulation as a character strength, which involves goal-setting, progress monitoring, and emotional and behavioural control. Through self-regulated learning, students develop persistence and resilience, which are vital skills for self-regulation in the contexts of everyday life. Although his research primarily targets academic settings, the strategies Barr promotes contribute to students' broader self-regulation development, helping them manage impulses and focus on long-term goals.

Understanding the distinctions and intersections between self-regulation as a character strength and as a self-regulated learner allows individuals to harness their strengths effectively, optimising both their personal growth and academic success. By doing so, they not only improve their learning and performance but also promote their wellbeing, creating a more balanced and fulfilling educational experience.

Table 13 outlines a range of activities, highlighting their benefits for learning and overall wellbeing, demonstrating how intentional engagement can enhance both cognitive development and personal flourishing.

Table 13: Enhancing learning and wellbeing through engaging activities

Activity	Benefits for wellbeing	Benefits for learning
Mindfulness and meditation	Reduces stress, enhances emotional awareness and improves focus	Improves concentration, helps manage academic stress and boosts cognitive performance
Journalling	Promotes emotional clarity, self-reflection and self-awareness, and reduces anxiety	Helps track academic progress, clarify thoughts, develop self-management skills and set learning goals
Goal-setting	Builds motivation, provides a sense of accomplishment and boosts self-confidence	Enhances focus on learning objectives, helps track progress and encourages persistence
Deep breathing	Lowers levels of stress, slows and calms the mind, and encourages emotional regulation	Increases focus, calmness and levels of anxiety when facing pressures of assessment

Self-regulation for neurodivergent students

Self-regulation, whether for wellbeing or learning, also emphasises the importance of motivation and perseverance in the face of challenges, which are critical factors in maintaining a positive and healthy mindset. For neurodivergent students, who may find managing cognitive and emotional challenges more difficult, developing skills to self-regulate can be very beneficial. Goal-setting and planning can assist neurodivergent students to break tasks down into manageable steps, reducing overwhelming feelings and fostering a greater sense of control and calm. By defining clear goals and creating action plans, neurodivergent students can gain a sense of direction in both their academic and personal lives, which is essential for their overall wellbeing.

Teaching neurodivergent students to track their progress and reflect on their experiences helps them develop a better understanding of their learning processes and emotional states. This helps them cope with challenges and build on strengths, contributing to their emotional resilience and mental health.

Additionally, developing self-control and emotional regulation through impulse control techniques and emotional awareness exercises can help these students recognise and manage their emotions in various situations. This results in improved regulation and calmer interactions with others and a greater ability to focus on tasks, which enhances their social wellbeing and academic success.

Building motivation and persistence is also crucial; encouraging a growth mindset and providing positive feedback can help students stay motivated and resilient in the face of difficulties, fostering a positive outlook on life and learning. Moreover, implementing effective learning and wellbeing strategies, such as mindfulness and healthy lifestyle habits, provides neurodivergent students with tools to balance their academic and personal commitments, supporting their holistic wellbeing.

By fostering a supportive environment and integrating self-regulation practices into the curriculum, educators can help neurodivergent students enhance their learning experiences and overall wellbeing, leading to greater success and fulfillment in their lives.

Activity: Developing self-regulation for learning and wellbeing

Make goal-setting for wellbeing and learning, using SMART or WOOP goals, part of your classroom routine.

Monday morning

Have students set a wellbeing goal for the day/week. For example:

- Practise gratitude daily
- Create a new social connection in the yard
- Focus on what triggers different emotions throughout the day.

Have students set a learning goal for the day/week. This could include something related to:

- Acquiring knowledge or skills
- Developing a study habit
- Critical thinking/analysis
- Creativity/innovation.

Tuesday, Wednesday and Thursday mornings

Set aside five minutes to review the wellbeing and learning goals:

- Explore progress and obstacles
- Recognise and articulate distractions
- Reframe goals if needed.

Friday afternoon

Set aside time to review students' progress and experiences across the week:

- Individual reflection on successes, challenges and opportunities
- Share with a partner/the whole group
- Celebrate achievements
- Acknowledge challenges.

Student agency and wellbeing

The concept of student agency has become very important in education. It means that students should have the power to make choices and decisions about their learning. By using methods that boost student agency, teachers can create learning environments where students do well academically and also feel better mentally, emotionally and socially, ultimately improving their wellbeing.

Facilitating student agency involves empowering students with the autonomy to set their own learning goals, choose their learning paths and engage in activities that reflect their interests and needs. It is based on the belief that when students have a sense of ownership over their learning, they are more motivated, engaged and likely to succeed.

Key aspects of student agency include:

- **Choice and autonomy:** Students have the opportunity to make decisions about their learning, such as selecting topics of interest, choosing methods of learning and determining the pace of their progress.
- **Voice and participation:** Students are encouraged to express their opinions, ask questions and participate actively in discussions and decision-making processes.
- **Goal-setting:** Students are guided to set realistic and achievable goals for themselves, fostering a sense of purpose and direction in their learning journey.
- **Reflection and self-assessment:** Students are taught to reflect on their learning experiences, assess their progress and identify areas for improvement.

The connection between student agency and wellbeing

The link between student agency and wellbeing is important and has been explored by many researchers. When students have control over their learning, they tend to develop a stronger sense of self, improve their emotional resilience and enhance their social skills.

Giving students a voice in their learning increases their level of motivation and their engagement with school and learning. When students make choices about what and how they learn, they develop a natural motivation and become more interested and involved. This helps them enjoy learning more and reduces the stress and anxiety that can come about as a result of more traditional and rigid approaches to education.

Student agency helps build self-efficacy. When students make decisions and see the results of their efforts, particularly if they had obstacles to overcome, there is a positive effect on their mental and emotional wellbeing and they gain further confidence in their own abilities.

Additionally, by taking charge of their learning, students learn to deal with challenges and setbacks more effectively and thus improve their emotional resilience. They begin to see difficulties as opportunities for growth rather than barriers that can't be overcome.

Student agency also strengthens social connections. When students work together on projects and share ideas, they build better relationships with their peers. This teamwork helps create a stronger sense of community and support within the classroom context.

Allowing students to control their learning can reduce stress and anxiety as they can feel less pressure from external evaluations and fear of failure. This autonomy makes the learning environment more relaxed and supportive, helping students focus on learning without excessive stress.

To enhance student agency in the classroom you can:

- **Provide a flexible learning environment:** Create a classroom setup that allows for flexibility in seating, grouping and learning activities. There may be options for individual, group or whole-class learning that caters to individual learning styles and preferences.
- **Offer choice and a range of activities:** Provide students with a variety of options for assignments, projects and activities through choice boards or learning menus. This allows students to select tasks that align with their interests and strengths.
- **Develop student-led conferences:** Encourage students to take the lead in parent-teacher interviews or classroom presentations. This empowers them to discuss their progress, set goals and reflect on their learning experiences.
- **Include project-based learning:** Implement project-based learning approaches that allow students to explore real-world problems and develop solutions. This method promotes critical thinking, creativity and collaboration among students. Often referred to as passion projects, these work to develop skills such as grit, critical thinking, problem-solving and creativity.

- **Build a culture of feedback and reflection:** Provide regular opportunities for students to give and receive feedback related to their learning and wellbeing goals. Encourage them to reflect on their experiences, assess their progress and identify any obstacles preventing them from achieving their goals.
- **Make decision-making collaborative:** Involve students in classroom decisions, such as setting classroom rules, choosing topics for study or planning events. This participation fosters a sense of ownership and responsibility among students, while establishing a clearer understanding of purpose.

By empowering students to take control of their learning, educators can foster a positive and supportive learning environment where students thrive academically, emotionally and socially. As we continue to explore and implement strategies that promote student agency, we pave the way for a more engaging, meaningful and fulfilling educational experience for all students.

Challenges and considerations

While acknowledging that student agency offers numerous benefits, including that it can be a powerful tool for enhancing student wellbeing, we must also validate the potential challenges educators may face in its implementation.

As educators, we understand that a 'one-size-fits-all' model does not work. In introducing more agency to the classroom we may face resistance from students who are more suited to a traditional teacher-centred approach. How would we cater to their needs while ensuring their voices are being heard? How can we work to strike a balance between providing autonomy and ensuring both rigour and accountability?

To address these challenges, educators could:

- **Provide guidance and support:** Offer clear guidelines and scaffolding to help students make informed decisions. Gradually increase the level of autonomy as students become more comfortable with the concept of agency.
- **Promote a growth mindset:** Encourage a growth mindset among students by emphasising the value of effort, persistence and learning from mistakes. This mindset helps students embrace challenges and view setbacks as opportunities for growth.

- **Foster a positive classroom culture:** Create a classroom environment that values diversity, inclusivity and respect. Encourage open communication and collaboration, allowing students to feel safe and supported in expressing their ideas and opinions.

In summary, student agency is crucial for enhancing student wellbeing. It boosts motivation, builds self-confidence, improves emotional resilience, strengthens social ties and reduces stress. When we provide students with more control over their learning, we can create a more effective and supportive environment that benefits the students' overall development.

CHAPTER 8
SUPERCHARGING STUDENT WELLBEING
Responsive Strategies

Supercharge student wellbeing by responding appropriately, helping them stay safe online, creating powerful sharing circles, building in gameplay and developing service learning as student-focused moves.

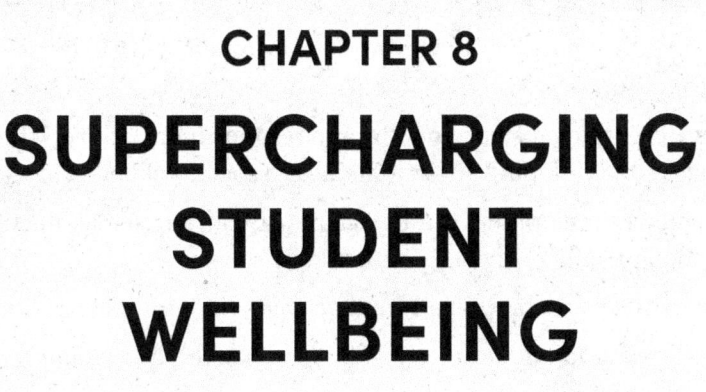

In this chapter we'll focus on practical strategies to enhance student wellbeing. We'll explore how:

- To create a supportive and positive environment, both in person and online.
- Service learning fosters empathy and responsibility, both of which are crucial for developing our emotional and social wellbeing.
- Character development through gameplay can be used as an engaging method to build resilience and self-awareness.
- Different types of praise and feedback has various impact on students.
- The different methods of feedback can enhance student confidence and motivation.
- Sharing circles can be used as a valuable tool for fostering open communication and trust – key components of a healthy, connected community.

Together, these strategies offer a comprehensive approach to promoting student wellbeing.

How we respond to our students matters

Praise is a powerful tool in education, parenting and leadership. It can motivate individuals, encourage growth and foster a positive environment. However, not all praise is created equal. Understanding the difference between effective praise and process praise can help individuals harness the benefits of praise while avoiding potential pitfalls. Additionally, incorporating active constructive responses into interactions can further enhance the impact of praise by strengthening relationships and building a positive feedback loop.

Effective praise, also known as specific praise, focuses on the individual's accomplishments, effort or behaviour with a specific outcome in mind. It is characterised by being:

- **Specific and detailed:** Effective praise targets specific actions or behaviours that you want to encourage. For example, instead of saying, 'Great job,' a teacher might say, 'I appreciate how you organised your essay with clear arguments and supporting evidence.'

- **Sincere and genuine:** The praise should be honest and reflective of the individual's true abilities or achievements. Insincere praise can be counterproductive and may lead to scepticism.
- **Goal-oriented:** Effective praise aligns with the individual's goals, whether they are learning objectives, personal development goals or completed tasks.
- **Timely:** Praise given soon after the accomplishment or behaviour reinforces the desired action, helping the individual make a clear connection between their effort and the praise.

These characteristics are particularly relevant in Australian contexts where the use of specific, authentic praise is often emphasised in educational settings to support student engagement and growth.

Process praise emphasises the effort and strategies used by an individual rather than the outcome. It is focused on how a task is approached rather than the result. Key characteristics of process praise include:

- **Focusing on effort:** Process praise highlights the hard work, persistence or dedication demonstrated by the individual. For example, 'I appreciate how you kept trying different methods to solve the maths problem.'
- **Emphasising strategies:** This type of praise encourages the use of effective strategies or problem-solving methods. For instance, 'Your decision to break down the task into smaller parts really paid off.'
- **Promoting a growth mindset:** Process praise helps foster a belief in one's ability to grow and improve through effort and learning.
- **Encouraging risk-taking:** By emphasising effort and learning, process praise reduces the fear of failure, encouraging individuals to take on challenges and try new things.

Australian educational research often supports the use of process praise, particularly in promoting a growth mindset among students. Research has shown that focusing on students' effort and perseverance rather than outcomes can lead to higher levels of motivation and engagement.

Active constructive responding

Active constructive responding (ACR) is a communication style that involves enthusiastically and positively engaging with someone's achievements or experiences. It can deepen relationships and enhance the impact of praise.

ACR is characterised by:

- **Listening and engaging:** Fully listening to the individual's story or achievement and engaging with them through positive, enthusiastic feedback.
- **Showing authentic interest:** Responding with genuine excitement and interest helps validate the individual's experience and creates a supportive atmosphere.
- **Engage with follow-up questions:** By asking questions about the experience, you show curiosity and encourage the person to share more details about their achievement.
- **Acknowledging positive emotions:** Recognising the individual's positive emotions associated with their experience can amplify the impact of praise and strengthen the relationship.

For example, when someone shares a success with you, instead of simply saying, 'That's great!' you could say, 'Wow, that's amazing! Tell me more about how you achieved that. How did it feel when you accomplished it?' Incorporating ACR is particularly effective in our educational settings, as it fosters open communication and positive relationships between members of the community.

In 2004, psychologist Shelly Gable and her team identified four possible responses we have to sharing good news: active-constructive, passive-constructive, active-destructive and passive-destructive (Gable et al. 2004; see table 14).

Table 14: The responses we may have to someone sharing good news

	Destructive	Constructive
Active	'Squashes' the good news, stifling the conversation.	Genuinely connects to the information. Shares in the joy. Amplifies the experience.
Passive	Takes over the conversation, ignores the news. Makes it about 'them'.	Lacking genuine interest with minimal support or backing, closing the conversation.

Source: Adapted from Gable et al., 2004.

Let's say, for example, a student approaches you to let you know they are going on an overseas family holiday Table 15 shows how you might respond according to Gable's theory.

Table 15: Example of the responses we may have to someone sharing good news

	Destructive	Constructive
Active	WOW. Really? You know that means you might miss out on school and learning. Won't you miss your friends? I'm really surprised you would want to do that. *Focuses on the negative details. Person may feel that the news wasn't good after all.*	How exciting! That's great news. You'll end up with so many new experiences and memories… very cool! Where are you going? *Elaborates the discussion and validates the person's feelings of joy.*
Passive	That's great news. But guess what? I am going overseas as well. I'll be visiting at least four countries in Europe. *Focus moves away from the person and onto yourself, making the focus about you and stopping the original conversation.*	That's great. *A statement that closes the conversation. Person may feel embarrassed sharing the news.*

Try role-playing the responses with students. Some example scenarios you could use include:

- They just passed their driving test and now have their licence.
- They bought a new game for their gaming console.
- They're going to their favourite restaurant for dinner.
- They played a really exciting game with their friends at lunchtime.
- They are finally getting to go on their dream holiday.

Effective feedback

Effective feedback is essential for helping individuals grow and develop. It can be achieved through a combination of effective praise, process praise and active constructive responding. Characteristics of effective feedback include:

- **Specific and actionable language:** Effective feedback focuses on specific actions or behaviours, providing clear guidance on what to continue or improve.
- **A balance:** Feedback should include both praise for strengths and constructive criticism for areas of improvement.
- **Timely delivery**: Providing feedback soon after an event or achievement ensures that it is relevant and allows for immediate adjustments.
- **Objective and non-judgemental language:** Feedback should be based on observable behaviour and avoid personal judgements.
- **A growth mindset:** Effective feedback encourages the individual to see challenges as opportunities for growth and emphasises the importance of effort and learning.
- **Opportunity for self-reflection:** Feedback should prompt individuals to reflect on their performance and identify areas for improvement.

Balancing effective praise, process praise and active constructive responding

Use effective praise to:

- Recognise a specific achievement or accomplishment.
- Motivate and reward the completion of an activity or reaching a goal.

Use process praise to:

- Encourage persistence and effort in challenging tasks.
- Focus on the individual's approach to solving problems or tasks.
- Nurture a growth mindset by emphasising learning and improvement.

Use active constructive responding to:

- Deepen relationships and foster trust through enthusiastic and positive engagement.
- Validate the individual's emotions and experiences, amplifying the impact of praise.

- Create a supportive and motivating environment that encourages sharing and connection.

Understanding when and how to use each type of communication can help to create a supportive environment that values both achievement and growth, leading to more confident, resilient and motivated students who are willing to take on challenges to achieve their goals.

Online safety for you and your students

In today's digital age, the internet is an integral component of our lives, offering opportunities for learning, socialisation and entertainment. However, with these benefits comes a range of significant risks to those who are not educated on how to remain safe online. This makes online safety curriculum crucial for schools to include as part of their wellbeing goals, strategies and framework.

When we speak of digital wellbeing we are referring to the impact technology has on our mental, emotional and physical health. Digital wellbeing involves maintaining a healthy relationship with technology, ensuring it enhances rather than detracts from our lives. This concept includes the ability to manage our health, safety, relationships and work-life balance in digital environments. We know that technologies can enhance our personal goals, our social interactions, our community engagement and our ability to learn new and exciting things. However, what is crucial is that, while we are engaging technology for all of these things, we are also using technology to positively support our emotional, psychological and physical health.

In her book *Sexts, Texts and Selfies* (2018), Australia's leading cyber safety expert, Susan McLean, explores how today's youth connect globally. She writes that young people are often unaware that their private posts can reach wider audiences, which may lead to negative outcomes. McLean educates staff and students about how cyberbullying and technology misuse are major non-academic challenges for schools and demand significant time, effort and resources. For some families, a lack of understanding around online safety has meant that the school's duty of care to address online issues has increased, requiring further staff education. With this in mind, schools should continue to embrace technology, while at the same time educating the community, maintaining updated policies and handling breaches efficiently and sensitively.

As discussed earlier, a whole-school approach, where explicit and implicit teaching is delivered, offers many benefits. In the world of digital and online safety education, this is no different. Developing a scope and sequence that begins at the start of schooling and addresses topics such as being a good digital citizen, distinguishing between real-life and online friends, and understanding rules for posting content online provides numerous benefits. It also includes maintaining personal safety, managing digital footprints and protecting digital reputations to foster responsible online behaviour that contributes to the creation of a safer and more supportive learning environment. Knowing that the boundaries between home and school are now blurred as a result of online connection, involving the whole-school community (teachers, students, parents and support staff) ensures a stronger form of protection where everyone is aware of online risks and equipped to manage them. This collective effort results in consistent messaging across all aspects of school life, reinforcing safe online behaviours and principles at every opportunity.

Becoming more aware of the constant advances in technology is also key. This can help to identify potential risks early and address them before they escalate. Students benefit from gaining critical digital literacy skills, empowering them to navigate the online world safely and respond effectively to dangers such as cyberbullying, grooming and exposure to inappropriate content. Engaging parents and the broader community ensures that the lessons learned at school are reinforced at home, creating a cohesive support system for students.

A whole-school approach should also be adaptive to emerging online threats, allowing schools to quickly update their policies and practices to protect students against new risks. The shared responsibility for online safety across the entire school community fosters a collaborative environment, where everyone contributes to maintaining a safe digital space. This approach also emphasises ongoing professional development for teachers and staff, ensuring they are well-equipped to guide students and handle online safety issues as they arise.

A whole-school approach also creates a culture of openness and support, encouraging students to speak up about any online issues they encounter, knowing they will receive help and guidance. By embedding online safety into the curriculum and daily activities, it becomes a natural part of students' learning experience, ensuring that digital literacy is recognised as an essential life skill.

Resources for online safety

- alannahandmadeline.org.au/resources/digital-citizenship-resources-digital-wellbeing
- commonsense.org/education/collections/digital-well-being-lessons-for-grades-k-12
- cybersafetysolutions.com.au
- esafety.gov.au/educators

How sharing circles can help students to thrive

There is consensus around the need for students to feel safe, heard, valued and supported within the school context – both in and out of the classroom. Providing them with the opportunity to openly discuss their thoughts and feelings is a great way to achieve this. Research is clear on the benefits of structured sharing circles or circle time and the ability these have to develop a clearer understanding of self, learning experiences and the creation of stronger relationships for students.

Sharing circles can be used in a number of ways:

- To introduce new topics and ideas
- To discuss our thoughts and feelings on particular topics and issues
- To share stories or items that they love or that make them feel good.

The benefits of sharing circles include:

- **A stronger sense of connection in the classroom:** Sharing circles help students connect with each other and their teachers. This sense of community makes students feel like they belong, which boosts their confidence and wellbeing. A strong community can make school a more enjoyable and supportive place for everyone.
- **A greater sense of empathy and understanding among students:** When students listen to their peers share their experiences, they begin to understand different perspectives. This builds empathy and helps students appreciate the diversity of opinions and backgrounds in the classroom, which is an important life skill.
- **Improved ability to manage emotions:** Sharing circles provide a safe space for students to talk about their emotions. By expressing their feelings, students can learn to recognise and manage them

more effectively. This can lead to healthier emotional responses and improved emotional intelligence.

- **Boosted confidence and levels of self-expression:** Sharing circles offer a structured way to talk about difficult topics the students may face such as: mental ill-health, mean-on-purpose behaviours, or friendship issues. Creating a safe space for these conversations allows students to learn from each other and promotes a more inclusive culture within the classroom.
- **Improved teamwork and a support network:** As students share their thoughts, they often find common ground with other students in the class. This can lead to natural support systems and collaborative efforts where students learn from each other and work together, which is beneficial both in and out of the classroom.
- **More self-awareness and reflection:** Sharing circles encourage students to think about their experiences and how their words and actions affect themselves and others. This reflection fosters self-awareness and personal growth, helping students become more mindful and considerate. They learn that their words and actions affect others as well as their understanding of self.

Table 16 shows how to ensure a feeling of a safe and secure environment within a sharing circle, using the acronym BREATHE.

Be sure to set clear guidelines for your sharing circles, such as:

- One person speaks at a time.
- Everyone listens.
- Prompts are used to guide you.
- You can pass, but we might come back and ask you again.
- Confidentiality is always respected.
- Respectful language is to be used.

Have a clear format and structure for your sharing circles:

- Have an introductory activity – a game, a book excerpt or a short clip – to act as a stimulus for the topic.
- Follow the guidelines to explore the topic or prompt.
- Have a closing activity that enables reflection – where students have the opportunity to share their thoughts and understandings of what has been shared.

Table 16: Promote active listening and a secure environment through BREATHE

B	Body language	Use eye contact, nodding and open posture to show engagement
R	Reflection	Paraphrase or summarise to confirm understanding
E	Empathy	Acknowledge and validate the speaker's emotions and perspective
A	Attention	Focus entirely on the speaker, avoiding distractions
T	Taking turns	Let the speaker finish without interrupting
H	Highlight	Retain key points for later reference and meaningful connections
E	Encouragement	Use verbal affirmations to keep the conversation flowing

Character development through gameplay

As Plato said, 'You can discover more about a person in an hour of play than in a year of conversation.' Traditional board games have been designed for years to stimulate both brain activity and enjoyment. They expose players to competition, organised rules and the opportunity to strategise through innovative, creative and critical thinking. In a school context, games can be used as a significantly more effective means of student engagement and involvement. They align closely with the General Capabilities of the Australian Curriculum as follows:

- **Critical and Creative Thinking:**
    - Analysing, synthesising and evaluating information
    - Reflecting on thoughts and actions
    - Generating innovative ideas and possibilities
    - Identifying, exploring and clarifying information

- **Personal and Social Capability:**
  - Self and social awareness
  - Self and social management
- **Ethical Understanding:**
  - Exploring values, rights and ethical principles
  - Understanding ethical concepts and issues
  - Reflecting on personal ethics in experiences and decision-making

As a school, it is important to provide experiences in which children can engage with strategic thinking games that, in turn, benefit their wellbeing. Simple observations of children playing clearly identifies character strengths at work through:

- **Increasing levels of creativity:**
  - Solving problems – making connections to the world around them and then applying their knowledge to similar situations
- **Promotion of curiosity:**
  - Risk-taking
- **Improved judgement:**
  - Planning and making decisions
  - Cognitive problem-solving
  - Investigating situations and exploring options
- **Improved self-regulation:**
  - Pausing and reflecting before making decisions
  - Short-term versus long-term strategies
- **Developing fairness:**
  - Being just in their moves
  - Demonstrating respect for their opponents
  - Demonstrating respect for the rules
- **Demonstrating humility:**
  - Learning to win with dignity and to lose with grace
  - Recognising opponents' effective strategies
- **Developing perspective:**
  - Being able to analyse an entire board and see it from many angles.

At Trinity College, SA, we have adopted both the Mind Lab and Accelium methodologies and platforms to help foster and promote these skills in our students. Mind Lab and Accelium use strategy games to develop higher-order cognitive, emotional and social skills through play. Structured game-playing sessions, which are entertaining, engaging and exciting, enable students to learn life skills and deepen their creative and critical thinking capabilities.

Mind Lab Classic adopts a hands-on approach, while Accelium, Mind Lab's most recent response to the agile needs of students and schools, incorporates the art of digital learning. Both approaches involve the introduction of a metacognitive model whereby students analyse emotional and cognitive processes all the while learning to develop, discuss, challenge and refine effective strategies that are transferable into real-world situations. Being actively engaged in these decisions helps children develop an increased ability to become better risk assessors as they learn to navigate a game board and calculate best strategies.

In an interview on The Jigsaw24 EdTech Podcast, Chris Ramsden, from Accelium and Mind Lab Australia, sums up the transformative power of game-based learning. He says, 'Use the game as the provocation to get into the cognitive, social, emotional and ethical skills, while developing strategies, teasing out and teaching metacognitive models of teaching which the kids can then use to transfer into real life' (Foote, 2024).

Students love being involved in games-based education projects. Here is what some of them have said:

- 'It is good because some times you have to stop and look back at the board and see what options are available to you and then you have to weigh up the best choice.'
- 'In my game you have resources and you learn that you just don't go out and use all your resources at once because later on you might be stuck and you could have used them then.'
- 'I have to use my strength of prudence so that I am aware of what I am doing and not just doing anything without thinking about it first.'

The benefits of service learning

Service learning offers a range of benefits to students' wellbeing and the community. When we deliver an authentic approach to service, we create a meaningful way for students to develop their levels of compassion, foster hope and promote justice. We provide opportunities for them to contribute to the creation of more caring and connected communities. But what do we mean when we speak of service learning?

Service learning is an educational approach that integrates a student's academic journey with meaningful connection to provide service to someone beyond themselves. The process enables students to apply classroom theories to real-world problems, often in collaboration with non-profit or social service organisations. The approach involves a continuous cycle of action, reflection and critical thinking, aimed at deepening students' understanding of academic content while fostering civic responsibility. Unlike traditional volunteerism, which primarily focuses on service, service learning equally emphasises both learning and service. This methodology not only enhances students' practical skills and knowledge but also nurtures their growth as active citizens, contributing to both their personal development and that of their communities. By addressing community needs through service projects that are seamlessly integrated into the curriculum, service learning prepares students to engage with and solve societal challenges in the 21st century.

Core components of service learning include:

- **Community engagement:** The heart of service learning lies in its connection to the community. Students work on projects that have real impact, addressing genuine community needs. This direct engagement fosters a sense of responsibility and civic duty.
- **Academic integration:** Service learning is not an extracurricular activity; it is integrated into the curriculum. Projects are tied to academic objectives, ensuring that students not only contribute to the community but also enhance their learning in areas such as critical thinking, problem-solving and subject-specific knowledge.
- **Reflection:** Reflection is a crucial element of service learning. Students are encouraged to think critically about their experiences, discuss the outcomes and connect their service with academic and personal growth. This reflective practice helps them internalise the lessons learned and apply them to future situations.
- **Collaboration:** Service learning often involves collaboration among students, teachers and community partners. This teamwork helps students develop social skills, learn from different perspectives and build stronger community ties.

Service learning has a profound impact on student wellbeing, offering benefits that extend beyond the classroom. These benefits can be categorised into several key areas:

- **Emotional wellbeing:**
    - **Having a sense of purpose:** Engaging in service learning helps provide students with a sense of purpose and fulfillment. When they contribute to meaningful projects it allows them to see the tangible results of their efforts, in turn boosting their self-esteem and emotional wellbeing.
    - **Developing empathy and compassion:** When they work on projects that address the needs of their community, students develop empathy and compassion through the deeper understanding gained of the challenges others face, leading to greater emotional resilience and a more positive outlook on life.

- **Social wellbeing:**
    - **Building a stronger community connection:** Service learning strengthens students' connection to their community. Working alongside community members and peers helps students develop a sense of belonging and an understanding of the importance of teamwork and collaboration.
    - **Building stronger relationships:** The collaborative nature of service learning helps students build strong relationships with their peers, teachers and members of their school and local community. These relationships are important when it comes to needing social support – a key component of wellbeing.

- **Mental wellbeing:**
    - **Learning to think critically and problem-solve:** Service learning projects often involve exploring complex challenges requiring creative solutions. Through this, students enhance their critical thinking and problem-solving skills, contributing to their cognitive development and mental resilience.
    - **Learning to reduce stress:** Participating in service learning can also reduce stress through the act of helping others and contributing to a greater good. This can provide a sense of satisfaction and reduce feelings of anxiety or helplessness.

- **Physical wellbeing:**
  - **Active engagement:** Many service learning projects involve physical activity, whether it is cleaning up a local park or cemetery, building a community garden, or engaging to organise a fundraising event. These physical activities promote health and wellness, contributing to students' overall physical wellbeing.
- **Academic wellbeing:**
  - **Enhancing student learning:** The practical application of classroom knowledge in service learning projects reinforces academic concepts, leading to better retention and understanding. This can result in improved academic performance and a greater sense of achievement.
  - **Increased engagement and levels of motivation:** Students often find service learning more engaging than traditional classroom activities as it connects with them on an emotional level. This increased engagement may lead to a more positive attitude towards learning and greater motivation to pursue academic success.

Ultimately, service learning is a powerful tool that educators can use to enhance academic learning and promote wellbeing in various dimensions. By engaging in meaningful community service, students develop a sense of purpose, build strong relationships, enhance their critical thinking skills and improve their physical and emotional health. As educators, integrating service learning into the curriculum offers a holistic approach to education, preparing students not just for academic success, but for a fulfilling and compassionate life.

CHAPTER 9
CREATING A TRAUMA-INFORMED CLASSROOM
Intentional Practices for Lasting Habits and Goals

Through intentional wellbeing practices, we create a trauma-informed classroom where wellbeing is visible, habits flourish and goals come to life.

Bringing all of the elements of the previous chapters together, we can now explore how our wellbeing practices can significantly impact the social, physical and emotional health and development of our community members – staff, students and parents. When we build in practices that promote strategies for awareness of our emotional state of mind and respond accordingly, where we develop regular habits to enhance our wellbeing through daily practices, and when we have skills to help form positive relationships, we are able to help shift our thinking into a more positive sphere.

Wellbeing practices help us authentically demonstrate how we look after the wellbeing of ourselves and others. They move beyond the teaching of programs and activities that develop wellbeing, rather now showing how we can embed these skills into our lives through daily practices.

Making wellbeing visible

The Visible Wellbeing framework developed by Professor Lea Waters offers schools and educators a practical, evidence-based approach to help make wellbeing a core part of educational practices and processes. It goes beyond focusing on academic achievement in an attempt to nurture the psychological and emotional development of students and staff. The significance of the framework is its ability to make the *invisible* – students' emotional, social and psychological experiences – *visible*, allowing these crucial elements of wellbeing to be recognised, nurtured and integrated into daily life and learning practices.

One of the simplest language tools that can help to make wellbeing visible is the See, Hear, Feel practice – a key part of the Visible Wellbeing framework. It is designed to help us become more aware of wellbeing by tuning into our own and others' emotional and mental states in everyday life. The practice encourages paying mindful attention to different aspects of wellbeing, making it more visible and tangible, as follows:

- **See:** Pay attention to the physical signs of wellbeing. This could involve observing body language, facial expressions and behaviour that indicate how someone is feeling; for instance, noticing if students are slumped in their chairs or smiling and energised.
- **Hear:** Listen to the verbal and non-verbal cues. This includes not only what is being said but also how it is being said (tone of voice, pitch, pace, choice of words). It is about tuning into conversations or sounds in the environment that may signal wellbeing or distress, including

those sounds that can be heard that aren't words (sniggers, huffs, items being slammed down).
- **Feel:** Tune into the emotional atmosphere and internal sensations. This involves reflecting on one's own emotional state and noticing feelings in the body (such as tension, relaxation or excitement) as well as the emotions present in others. These emotions can connect our body sensations to our mind and can often be expressed through sayings that we have developed over time, such as feeling hot under the collar, having butterflies in our stomach or having the weight of the world on our shoulders.

For years, teachers have used their senses to recognise how students are faring. However, by using this specific practice and articulating what you see, what you hear and how you feel, educators and students alike can build awareness of wellbeing, making it more visible and actionable in the classroom. The practice aims to enhance emotional literacy, mindfulness and self-regulation, creating a supportive environment for wellbeing to flourish. It also provides license for staff and students to acknowledge and validate their different states of emotional being and work through them; as the saying goes, if you can name it, you can tame it.

Unveiling the invisible

Emotions are often considered fleeting and not concrete. However, they can significantly affect how students engage with learning, how they interact with each other, and the approach they take to challenges they face. If we ignore the 'invisibility' of emotional wellbeing it can lead to missed opportunities to work with young people on strategies for early intervention, for understanding our range of emotions and emotional growth, and for the development of resilience.

Professor Lea Waters recognises that if we want to foster holistic development in students, we must first make the invisible visible. This means identifying, measuring and supporting the emotional and psychological states that have impact on learning. By making emotions and wellbeing visible, educators can respond proactively, creating environments where students feel emotionally safe and supported, ultimately being authentic to their emotional state.

The Visible Wellbeing framework brings emotions to the surface, ensuring that educators can observe, assess and cultivate students' emotional health in real time. This structured approach validates that our emotional state takes many forms throughout the day. It draws attention and awareness to our state of being and provides additional resources for our wellbeing toolkits.

Core components of the Visible Wellbeing framework

The framework is designed around key components that allow educators to transform the invisible world of emotions into something visible and actionable.

Waters describes wellbeing as multifaceted, involving emotional, social, physical, psychological and intellectual dimensions. The six pathways – strengths, emotional management, attention and awareness, relationships, coping and habits and goals (SEARCH – see table 17) – provide teachers with different lenses to identify and address wellbeing in their classrooms. By making these pathways explicit, educators can guide students to recognise their emotions and understand how they affect their learning, relationships and overall development.

Table 17: SEARCH – the six pathways of Visible Wellbeing

S	Strengths	Our strengths are who we are naturally as a person. They are enjoyable and help us to be our best self.
E	Emotional management	We need to understand our feelings so we can live well. If we can identify our feelings, we can learn how to manage them.
A	Attention and awareness	Attention is when we focus on ourselves, our emotions and how our body is feeling. Awareness means that we can pay attention to things as they happen.
R	Relationships	Having healthy friendships is important in our lives. We must learn how to have trust and respect in our relationships.
C	Coping	Being able to cope means that we can get through things that happen in our lives. Resilience helps us to bounce back when there are bad times.
H	Habits and goals	Habits are things we do without thinking about them – both good and bad. Goals help us plan to achieve something.

Tools for making wellbeing visible

The Visible Wellbeing framework provides educators with tools to make emotional states of wellbeing visible through daily classroom activities.

The Visible Wellbeing measurement tools are an essential component of making emotions more visible and measurable. The framework provides practical tools such as wellbeing surveys, mood trackers and classroom discussions to help students express their emotions. By tracking and assessing emotional states, educators can intervene when needed and adjust their teaching methods to better address the emotional needs of their students (collectively and individually).

Strength spotting is another vital tool in making the invisible visible. It involves making careful observations and commenting on character strengths as they are displayed by staff and students, reinforcing positive emotional experiences and fostering confidence. This not only highlights students' capabilities but also creates a culture of emotional visibility, where strengths and emotions are recognised and celebrated.

Another way to make wellbeing visible is through the development of wellbeing routines. These are designed to bring emotional awareness into daily lessons, making emotions more visible. They offer a chance to address issues early and integrate wellbeing into the learning process. We will look at some examples of these later in the chapter.

As discussed earlier, the wellbeing of educators is just as important as the wellbeing of our students. Teachers are role models in the classroom, and their emotional states have a significant influence on their students. The Visible Wellbeing framework recognises this and encourages educators to model emotional visibility. By being open about their own emotions and modelling self-regulation, teachers can help students learn how to manage their own emotions in healthy ways.

One simple way to keep this front of mind for staff is to have visual reminders (in obvious places for them, such as at the front of their daily planner) about what they do to look after their own wellbeing through each of the six pathways. For example:

- What do you do to become more aware of your feelings?
- What is a tool that you utilise as a coping strategy?
- What is something you do that reflects your character strengths?

Trauma-informed practices benefit all

A large part of this book has been about creating an environment that fosters students' holistic development to enable them to truly flourish. Since they spend most of their school day inside a classroom, it is obvious that the classroom environment must be one that nurtures their intellectual, emotional, social and psychological wellbeing. We have explored how a flourishing student feels connected to their community and is equipped with the skills to navigate the complexities of life. The Visible Wellbeing framework is one such example of providing an overarching scope to create a culture of belonging while developing emotional literacy, mindfulness, strengths, a growth mindset, resilience, engagement and meaning. Other frameworks can be designed, selected or contextually developed to suit the needs of your school or classroom environment. Whichever framework you implement, it's important to consider whether it is trauma informed.

It was previously considered that building trauma-informed practices into a classroom environment was crucial only for supporting students who may have experienced trauma. We now know that ensuring all students have a safe, supportive space to learn and thrive can profoundly impact every student's ability to engage, learn and flourish – not just those who have experienced trauma.

Since trauma can be hidden, it is essential for educators to approach all students with sensitivity, understanding that their behaviours may be influenced by their experiences, while creating an environment that is sensitive to all student needs. Trauma-informed classrooms focus on safety, trust, empowerment and emotional regulation. Isn't this good practice for all? We can utilise what is labelled as trauma-informed practices into the classroom to build thriving students.

My thriving classroom framework, pictured in figure 4, helps establish classroom practices that are trauma informed.

Figure 4 demonstrates how creating a supportive classroom begins with building strong, trusting relationships between students and teachers. Whether or not they've experienced trauma, when students feel valued and secure through positive interactions, they are more likely to thrive. Affirming communication strengthens the bonds between peers and staff. These practices help develop a sense of belonging, which is important for all, but particularly so for those who have experienced trauma.

Figure 4: The thriving classroom framework

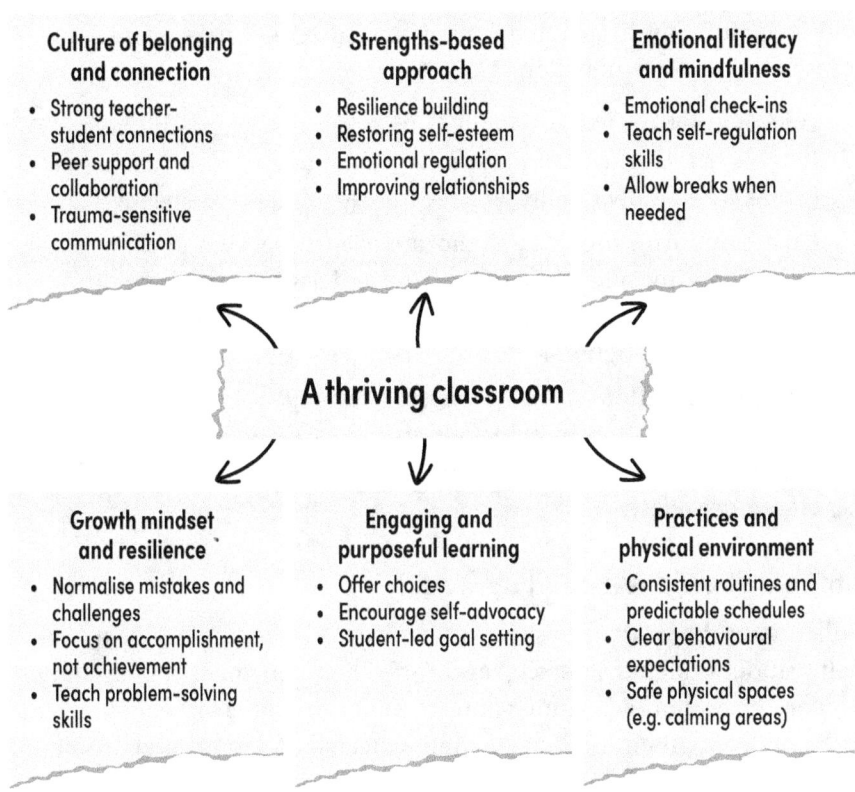

Through the use of character strengths, emotional literacy practices, purposeful tasks and goal-setting, we can help build resilience and confidence in students. Through the use of check-ins or mindfulness strategies to manage emotions, students are able to regain a sense of control when their emotions are heightened as well as a sense of ownership of their learning and wellbeing. Combine this with an environment that fosters consistent routines, displays schedules and sets clear expectations, and you create the foundation for nurturing both academic success and emotional wellbeing.

Let's talk through each part of the framework now.

Create a culture of belonging and connection

A classroom where students flourish begins with a sense of belonging. Students need to feel that they are valued members of the classroom community. When students experience a strong sense of connection to their peers and teachers, they are more likely to engage actively in learning and feel confident in taking academic and personal risks. Here's how to create a culture of connection:

- **Design practices that are inclusive:** Encourage diverse thinking relating to background and experience. Students should feel safe to express their individuality while respecting others' perspectives.
- **Create opportunities for collaborative learning:** Group work, peer mentoring and cooperative tasks and assignments help build social connections and foster teamwork, which benefits emotional development.
- **Design interactions to build a sense of empathy:** When teachers model empathy, they provide opportunities for every student to feel heard, understood and valued, thus strengthening their sense of emotional safety.

Utilise a strengths-based approach

Building on the work of positive psychology, a strengths-based approach helps students identify, develop and apply their personal strengths in both academic and non-academic contexts. When students are encouraged to focus on their strengths, they are more engaged and motivated, leading to better overall performance and increased life satisfaction. Teachers can promote strengths in the classroom by:

- **Helping students identify their strengths:** Through tools like reflection exercises, strength-based questionnaires or classroom discussions, students can begin to recognise their talents.
- **Creating opportunities for strength application:** Lessons and activities should be designed so students can apply their unique strengths in various scenarios, from problem-solving to creative tasks.
- **Celebrating all types of strengths:** Encourage diversity in strengths, ensuring students feel proud whether their strength is in leadership, creativity, empathy or resilience.

Build in practices of emotional literacy and mindfulness

Being equipped with emotional literacy provides students the ability to recognise, understand and manage their own emotions as well as the emotions of others. Being able to recognise and regulate their own emotional state is a key component of wellbeing and resilience, increasing students' ability to handle challenges, stress and frustration more effectively. In classrooms our emotional literacy should focus on:

- **Explicit teaching of emotional vocabulary:** Introducing students to a wide range of emotions and the language to express them, ensuring they are not limited to simple words such as 'happy' or 'sad'. Students need to develop an understanding of 'degrees' of emotion to drill down more accurately to what they are experiencing.
- **Mindfulness practices:** Integrating mindfulness exercises such as breathing techniques, quiet reflection of the school day or body scanning activities can help students develop self-awareness and increase levels of focus. Mindfulness can actively work to reduce anxiety and promotes emotional regulation, but should be treated as an individual benefit and not a 'one-size-fits-all' program.
- **Safe spaces for emotional expression:** Create opportunities where students can safely express and process their emotions. This could be through one-on-one conversations, journalling, or dedicated class discussions about feelings and experiences, such as the practice of circle time discussed earlier.

Aim to develop a growth mindset and sense of resilience

Understanding and accepting that challenges and setbacks are a natural part of learning and life helps students to flourish. Fostering a growth mindset – the belief that abilities can be developed through effort – is crucial to helping students persevere in the face of difficulties. Classrooms that promote resilience and a growth mindset often include:

- **Positive reinforcement of effort:** Instead of praising innate ability, teachers emphasise the importance of persistence, effort and learning from mistakes (as we discussed in chapter 3).
- **Normalising failure:** Create a classroom culture where mistakes are viewed as opportunities to grow. Encourage students to share their struggles and how they overcame them. Use role-playing to demonstrate and create opportunities to explore options.
- **A toolbox of coping strategies:** Helping students understand different strategies to cope with stressors that impact their emotional regulation.

Create tasks that are engaging and purposeful

Learning needs to be authentic, meaningful, engaging and connected to the student's interests and goals for them to thrive. Having meaning and purpose is a powerful driver of motivation. To cultivate purpose in the classroom, ensure you are cultivating:

- **Relevance to real-world experiences:** Design projects and lessons that connect to students' lives, interests and future goals. This could involve service learning, passion projects or real-world problem-solving.
- **Independence and choice:** To increase intrinsic motivation and responsibility, offer students some autonomy in their learning, allowing them to make choices about how they engage with the desired content.
- **Creativity and innovation:** Provide opportunities for creative expression and critical thinking through the exploration of tasks with multiple solutions, enabling out-of-the-box thinking.

Intentionally integrate wellbeing practices into the curriculum

Wellbeing should not be an add on but a core component of daily classroom life. Schools that embed wellbeing practices within the curriculum see more sustained engagement, higher academic performance and increased overall student happiness. Examples of these practices could include:

- **Regular wellbeing check-ins:** Regular emotional check-ins, such as a mood meter, morning mindfulness or circle time, provide opportunities for students to reflect on their mental state and set goals for working on their wellbeing throughout the day.
- **Include social-emotional learning (SEL) through all curriculum areas:** SEL programs explicitly teach skills such as empathy, communication, conflict resolution and emotional regulation. When built into other curriculum areas, their benefits are woven into the learning experience and they are not seen as isolated skills.
- **Catching the positive:** Use systems that encourage positive behaviour through recognition and reinforcement, such as gratitude walls, shout-outs for acts of kindness, or strength spotting exercises all work to emphasise the behaviours we wish to see, while at the same time making students feel valued for their efforts.

Consciously design your physical environment

The classroom's physical environment also plays a critical role in shaping wellbeing. A space that is calm, organised and conducive to learning can help students feel more focused and emotionally balanced. To create a flourishing environment:

- **Find ways to utilise natural lighting and calming aesthetics:** Maximise natural light and use calming colours such as soft or natural earthy tones. Ensure the space is clutter-free and organised.
- **Provide flexible seating options:** Allow students the flexibility to move around and choose seating that works for their learning style, whether that is traditional desks, standing desks or floor cushions.
- **Create a designated wellbeing zone:** Designate areas where students can take a break, engage in quiet reflection or use calming strategies such as reading a book or doing a mindfulness activity. 'Wellbeing huts' are a good option for students to take refuge or to engage in small group activities more privately.

When teachers create classrooms that prioritise the above (connection, strengths, emotional literacy, resilience and purposeful learning) they create an environment where students can thrive – not just as learners, but as individuals.

Teacher self-care and awareness

The role of the teacher is critical in establishing these practices in the classroom. We know that this work can be emotionally taxing. As we discussed in chapter 3, we must ensure that we are practising self-care and maintaining awareness of secondary trauma so that we can sustain our capacity to support students. Teachers should prioritise their own wellbeing by setting boundaries, seeking support and engaging in self-care activities to make it easier to support all students more effectively. Additionally, ongoing professional development in wellbeing and trauma-informed practices will deepen the understanding for teachers to stay attuned to student needs.

Putting it all together to form habits and routines

Habits and routines are essential for creating an environment in which students can thrive emotionally, socially and academically. For many students, the predictability and structure that routines provide acts as a foundation for reducing stress, fostering a sense of security and enhancing learning outcomes. In a classroom setting, where students are expected to navigate various challenges daily, implementing consistent habits and routines can be a powerful tool to support their overall wellbeing. It is important to understand why routines matter, how they contribute to student wellbeing, and how teachers can establish meaningful habits that help students flourish.

One of the most fundamental benefits of establishing habits and routines in the classroom is the sense of safety and security they provide. Particularly for students who are neurodivergent or may experience stress, trauma or anxiety, the predictability of routines helps them feel grounded and in control. Here are some of the ways routines can help:

- **Reduced anxiety:** When students know what to expect, this reduces the uncertainty that can contribute to feelings of anxiety. A predictable classroom routine reassures students, giving them confidence to focus on learning rather than worrying about what might come next.
- **Increased trust:** Consistent routines help students trust that their environment is stable and that their teacher is reliable. Trust is particularly important for students who may experience instability in their lives outside of school.
- **Greater emotional safety:** Routines allow students to feel emotionally safe because they have boundaries and clear expectations. Knowing the flow of the day gives students the emotional space to engage, take risks and participate in classroom activities.

Routine plays a crucial role in supporting students' cognitive functioning by minimising distractions and fostering a mindset conducive to learning. When routines are well-established, students can focus more on the lesson content rather than worrying about the next steps or procedures. Habits such as starting each lesson with a brief review, a mindfulness activity or a wellbeing and emotional check-in can streamline cognitive processes. This helps students shift into 'learning mode' more easily and frees up mental energy for complex tasks. Predictable routines also reduce distractions by eliminating uncertainty, allowing students to move smoothly from one activity to the next without constant redirection. This structure is especially helpful for transitions, supporting younger students or those with attention challenges to maintain their focus and concentration throughout the day.

Habits are powerful tools for shaping behaviour over time. In classrooms, routines can reinforce positive behaviour while establishing habits that contribute to long-term wellbeing and can play a crucial role in emotional regulation. In classrooms where students know what to expect, they can better manage their emotions, leading to a more peaceful and productive learning environment.

When we establish these habits and routines we need to understand the needs of our students. Not all daily habits or routines will work for all. Table 18 outlines some options that are easily adaptable to any classroom situation and that may work for you.

Table 18: Habit and routine examples

Early energiser	Start the day with an activity to promote physical wellbeing. Research shows the importance of physical activity for cognitive development. A three-minute, fast-paced activity can set the scene for increased focus and attention in class.
Morning check-in	Each morning students position their 'marker' on a scale of where their emotional level sits This can be done individually with a place card on each student's desk (teachers are able to scan the room to check zones) or collectively on a wall poster providing visibility for all students.
Daily goal setting	Spend three minutes each morning having students set a wellbeing goal they would like to achieve by the end of the day. For example, speak with someone in their class they wouldn't normally speak to, find a new space in the yard that promotes a positive feeling, catch themselves having a negative thought and have a reframe option available.
Transition time	Provide quiet time at the end of each activity throughout the day, giving students the opportunity to collect their thinking before moving on to the next task/activity. (Teachers should use a calm voice to round off the current task and give opportunity for students to regulate their emotions before moving on.)
What went well	A three-minute 'shout out' after recess and lunch breaks to help shift the focus to the positive experiences students had during break times.
Gratitude journal	At the end of each day have students reflect on three things that worked well for them throughout the day and why these were meaningful.

CHAPTER 10
UNLOCKING WELLBEING
Aligning Frameworks and Strategies for Lasting Success

Unlock the power of a wellbeing framework in your school. Maintain momentum in wellbeing strategies and seamlessly align them with ACARA standards, building a culture of hope and wellbeing that empowers both staff and students for lasting success.

When we're developing wellbeing strategies in schools, we often feel an energy, a connection, a buzz and a sense of common purpose. We start the journey together and we are committed to seeing it through. However, as with any initiative, maintaining momentum becomes the greatest challenge. In fact, one of the questions I am most often asked is: 'How do you maintain the level of momentum created at the start of the journey?'

Keeping the momentum going, for any initiative, requires a process of flexibility, continuity, consistency and celebration. We have to keep front of mind that our school-based wellbeing strategy is an ever-evolving program, not a one-off event. We must develop our own sense of grit to maintain our passion and dedication to creating a culture where wellbeing practices remain effective and meaningful throughout the school year; where our staff and students are part of an environment where wellbeing skills and concepts are woven into daily routines; and where we are responsive to changing needs.

One of the main keys to success is to remain kind to ourselves! We are our own harshest critics, and we sometimes find it difficult to give due credit to how far we have travelled. This is particularly true when our wellbeing strategies become embedded into practice and are habitual and part of the ethos and culture of the school. They simply become part of the school's DNA, and it is only when we remove ourselves, or have someone with fresh eyes looking at what we do, that we can see how far we've come. This is why we must acknowledge every success we have along the way, because they form part of the journey we've travelled and can reflect on.

If you have been strategic in developing your wellbeing strategy, and it aligns with your school's values, your students' needs and the context in which your school is placed, that is a great start. If you have also ensured your staff have a clear understanding of the importance of your strategy and the meaning and purpose behind its implementation, you have created a basis that makes maintaining long-term commitment and passion easier.

Figure 5 shows some of the ways you can maintain momentum with staff and students.

Figure 5: Maintaining momentum with wellbeing

- Celebrate success
- Flexible and adaptive
- Role model
- Support and collaboration
- Maintain culture
- Habits and routines
- Reflect and feed back
- Strong foundation
- Maintain balance

Maintaining momentum with wellbeing

Strong foundation

The effectiveness of your wellbeing strategy, and the ability to maintain momentum, starts with the foundational elements that were laid early on. If staff are involved in the strategic development process, considering values, context and needs, and if they clearly understand the purpose behind the strategies, there is a greater chance for long-term engagement.

Habits and routines

Incorporating wellbeing strategies into daily routines is crucial for sustaining momentum. Small practices, such as mindfulness, gratitude and check-ins, become instinctive when they are integrated into school life. Setting these routines (which are intentional but not time-consuming) emphasises the importance of wellbeing, allowing teachers and students the opportunity to regulate and recharge.

Support and collaboration

When educators have shared experiences, they create stronger connections and are more likely to flourish. Having professional learning communities (PLCs) where interested groups can focus on wellbeing will also help maintain momentum. Actively discussing strategies, challenges and successes brings about a greater sense of connection. Additionally, bringing in guest (expert) speakers to address particular concepts/initiatives or provide another perspective can be beneficial for staff and help them feel supported knowing that they are not expected to be the keepers of all knowledge.

Flexible and adaptive

Our wellbeing strategies must be flexible, adaptive and evolve over time based on our community's needs. Being flexible and open to change is part of this. This means that regular assessment of current practices should be part of your strategy to enable necessary modifications, making sure that all practices remain effective and engaging. Giving yourself permission to stop if something feels like it is not working, and change direction if you need to, ensures you are responsive to student, staff and community needs.

Celebrate success

When we focus on our accomplishments and celebrate our progress, this serves as incentive to maintain momentum. We recognise that small wins and growth, not perfection, should be celebrated. This helps create a positive atmosphere, reinforcing the value of wellbeing strategies.

Role model

When staff act as role models, this helps maintain momentum. Students observe their teachers and support staff demonstrating wellbeing strategies (coping, emotional regulation, mindfulness and so on). When we normalise conversations about our feelings, we work towards creating a culture that gives license to people to have conversations around mental health.

Maintain culture

A unified approach, where all staff collaborate to make wellbeing practices part of the school's ethos, policies and co-curricular programs, makes wellbeing more sustainable. Leaders should ensure time is allocated for wellbeing events, both learning and experiential, making it clear that wellbeing is for all members of the school community.

Reflect and feed back

Being able to stop, analyse and reflect on your practices and your own wellbeing is an important way to effectively feed back and promote continual improvement. Self-forgiveness during the reflection process will allow you to validate your intentions, even when you feel you may not have been successful. When done authentically, this process helps motivate staff and students to take more ownership over their wellbeing.

Maintain balance

As teachers we want to do it all! We have such amazing intentions to provide the best for our students. However, we need to make sure that we also consider a balanced approach – where we are realistic about our limitations around time, energy and other commitments. Having a clear direction on significant strategies means the ability to implement them well and without additional pressure on ourselves.

In short, when asked, 'How do I maintain momentum?' my answer is straightforward: focus on sustainable strategies that align with your values, can be authentically integrated into your school setting, and allow yourself grace for moments that may not go as planned.

Bringing it all together

Let's go full circle back to where we started in chapter 1: the Australian Student Wellbeing Framework (ASWF). This framework is based on evidence connecting wellbeing and learning and was created to support schools to provide a strong foundation for students to flourish. There are various other wellbeing frameworks available, too, and it's useful to query how these align with the ASWF when we're using them in schools.

The two main frameworks I have explored in this book are Martin Seligman's PERMA model and Lea Waters' SEARCH framework, because they offer complementary, research-backed approaches to holistic student wellbeing. PERMA emphasises core elements of flourishing and provides a broad framework for both emotional and academic success. SEARCH adds a strengths-based focus on emotional regulation, resilience and coping skills, offering practical strategies for daily wellbeing. Together, they create a well-rounded approach for nurturing resilient, engaged and thriving students.

While this is true, it is important to note that other frameworks are available and could be considered for your environment, based around your context.

These include: 5 Ways To Wellbeing; Mind Matters; Be You; Flourishing at School; Positive Education (initiated through Geelong Grammar); and CASEL (Collaborative for Academic, Social, and Emotional Learning).

Table 19 provides a breakdown of how easily the three frameworks – the ASWF, SEARCH and PERMA – can be linked together or used individually to support holistic wellbeing in students. As they are frameworks and not a curriculum, schools have scope to integrate programs, initiatives and curricula from a wide range of sources.

Table 19: Linking frameworks

Wellbeing domain	ASWF	PERMA	SEARCH
Positive relationships	Encourages inclusion, diversity and student voice to build positive relationships	Relationships are key to flourishing	Emphasises building strong, supportive and meaningful relationships
Connection: All frameworks stress the importance of relationships for student wellbeing, inclusion and connection.			
Emotional wellbeing	Supports safe, respectful environments that help students regulate emotions	Positive emotions are essential to wellbeing	Focuses on emotional management and effective emotional regulation
Connection: All emphasise the need to cultivate emotional wellbeing through positive environments and emotional regulation.			
Engagement and coping	Provides safe spaces for students to engage and build resilience	Engagement in meaningful activities is a pillar of flourishing	Emphasises coping skills and resilience-building strategies
Connection: All support engagement in meaningful activities while enhancing coping and resilience skills.			

Wellbeing domain	ASWF	PERMA	SEARCH
Meaning and strengths	Promotes student agency, voice and purpose	Meaning and purpose are critical to wellbeing	Using strengths helps students find their purpose and direction
Connection: Finding purpose through using strengths (SEARCH) and meaningful engagement (PERMA) reinforces ASWF's student voice approach.			
Accomplishment and goals	Encourages students to set and achieve personal goals within a supportive environment	Accomplishment contributes to a sense of competence and success	Focuses on developing positive habits and setting meaningful goals
Connection: Promotes goal-setting and achievement, which builds resilience and personal accomplishment across all three frameworks.			
Student agency and voice	Student participation, choice and autonomy	Meaning and purpose	Strengths and engagement
Connection: Giving students a voice in their wellbeing and learning journey, promoting self-efficacy.			
Cultural and social diversity	Emphasises inclusion, respect and diversity	Relationships	Building relationships in a diverse context
Connection: Promoting understanding and respect for different cultural and social backgrounds.			

Linking a wellbeing framework to the ACARA standards

Table 20 will help you identify the links between a wellbeing culture and Australian Curriculum, Assessment and Reporting Authority (ACARA) standards. The examples demonstrate how authentic connections between ACARA and a wellbeing framework can be made without requiring significant change to practice.

Table 20: Links between ACARA standards and a wellbeing culture

ACARA standards	Links and examples
Positive emotions and emotional management align closely with the **Personal and Social Capability** strand, particularly in understanding and managing emotions, self-awareness and self-management.	**Health and Physical Education:** Students describe the influence that relationships and emotions have on their own and others' health and wellbeing. They apply strategies to promote positive interactions and identify the impact of emotions on behaviours. *Link to wellbeing: Incorporating activities such as gratitude journalling or mindfulness exercises helps students identify and regulate emotions, enhancing their emotional wellbeing.* **Personal and Social Capability (Self-Awareness):** Students identify and explain their emotional responses in different situations and apply strategies to manage their emotions. *Link to wellbeing: Teaching emotional regulation techniques, such as reflection on positive experiences, aligns with building positive emotions and fostering resilience.* **Example activities:** Activities such as a gratitude wall allow students to describe and apply emotional management techniques using reflective practices. Embed times to focus attention and awareness of emotional state to allow students to recognise and describe emotional changes while acknowledging the impact on themselves and the classroom climate.

ACARA standards	Links and examples
Being engaged or in flow aligns with the **Critical and Creative Thinking** capability, which encourages deep, meaningful engagement through inquiry, problem-solving and fostering curiosity.	**Science:** Students plan and conduct investigations, select appropriate methods, collect and record data and describe observations. *Link to wellbeing: By fostering inquiry-based learning and deep engagement with scientific experiments, students enter a state of flow, actively engaging in learning.* **Critical and Creative Thinking:** Students generate and evaluate ideas and consider alternatives. They seek solutions to challenges and persist with problem-solving. *Link to wellbeing: Cognitive engagement is fostered when students are involved in solving problems and working through challenges.* **Example activities:** Science: Students can engage in extended project-based learning, exploring passion-based topics and fostering deep engagement with the curriculum (meeting the Achievement Standards for scientific inquiry). Mathematics: Real-world problem-solving projects encourage persistence and critical thinking, aligned with the Achievement Standards.

ACARA standards	Links and examples
Relationships are essential to the **Personal and Social Capability** strand, focusing on social awareness, social management and respectful relationships.	**Health and Physical Education:** Students identify strategies to manage relationships and analyse the impact of relationships on wellbeing. *Link to wellbeing: Programs that teach empathy and conflict resolution help students build and sustain positive relationships, directly linking to the Health and Physical Education standards.* **Personal and Social Capability (Social Awareness and Social Management):** Through group work and collaboration, students learn how their behaviours and interactions impact other people. They develop awareness of their role in the group. *Link to wellbeing: Providing opportunities to develop healthy relationships through collaboration and communication works to meet the Achievement standard.* **Example activities:** Operating a buddy program or setting up student representative groups enhances collaboration and leadership, allowing students to demonstrate social management and collaboration skills.

ACARA standards	Links and examples
Ethical Understanding helps students explore values, purpose and the impact of their actions on others and society, fostering meaning and linking to Civics and Citizenship through societal contribution.	**Humanities and Social Sciences:** Students evaluate the significance of historical events, analyse the consequences, and reflect on their impact on contemporary society. *Link to Wellbeing: Exploring the meaning behind historical events fosters deeper understanding and connects students to a larger purpose, helping them see their role in society.*
	Ethical Understanding (Year 9/10): Students evaluate ethical concepts and apply ethical understanding in decision-making and actions that affect others. *Link to wellbeing: Meaning is fostered when students explore ethical dilemmas, connecting their decisions to broader societal impact and moral considerations.*
	Example activities: In Humanities and Social Sciences, students can engage in projects where they research and present on the significance of historical figures who created lasting societal change, linking to Achievement Standards about evaluating the significance of events and finding meaning in history. Ethical debates in English or Humanities and Social Sciences about modern global issues (such as climate change or human rights) allow students to apply ethical understanding and reflect on their actions' larger societal impact, fostering meaning.

ACARA standards	Links and examples
Personal and Social Capability encourages skill development in setting and achieving goals, resilience and achievement.	**Mathematics:** Students solve problems using multiple strategies, justify their solutions, and apply their understanding of mathematical concepts in a range of contexts. *Link to wellbeing: Promoting a growth mindset and recognising effort helps develop perseverance and a sense of accomplishment.*
	The Arts: Students plan and create artworks and reflect on their choices, demonstrating skills and improvement over time. *Link to wellbeing: Through artistic expression and the mastery of skills, students develop a sense of accomplishment as they see their progress.*
	Example activities: Goal-setting for solving increasingly challenging problems in Mathematics meets the Achievement Standard related to persistence and problem-solving while encouraging a growth mindset. Through Visual Arts, students can work on portfolios where they track their skill development and reflect on their growth, aligning with standards related to skill mastery and accomplishment.

ACARA standards	Links and examples
General Capabilities integration In addition to specific Learning Areas, the General Capabilities in the Australian Curriculum offer a broad framework for embedding a wellbeing model.	**Personal and Social Capability:** This capability is deeply aligned with all aspects of wellbeing, particularly in the areas of self-awareness, emotional regulation, goal-setting, building relationships and self-management. **Critical and Creative Thinking:** Encouraging students to think critically and creatively fosters engagement in learning, especially when students face meaningful problems. **Ethical and Intercultural Understanding:** Both of these capabilities help students connect to meaning by exploring their own values, as well as those of others and understanding how their actions contribute to the greater good.

The Australian Curriculum lends itself to weaving throughout a wellbeing framework that goes beyond the Personal and Social Capability and Health and Physical Education strands. For example, PERMA and SEARCH will authentically weave into various General Capabilities and Learning Areas such as Science, Mathematics, the Arts, Humanities and Social Sciences and English. This helps educators holistically develop students' academic skills while also nurturing their wellbeing. This multifaceted approach ensures that students are thriving emotionally, beyond learning content, by embedding wellbeing practices into the curriculum, enhancing academic outcomes and supporting both student and staff wellbeing, fostering a thriving school environment.

Creating a PERMA culture

In a practical sense, creating a PERMA culture offers another opportunity to maintain momentum as it embeds wellbeing practices by fostering positive emotions, engagement, relationships, meaning and accomplishment. The PERMA model, discussed throughout this book, offers opportunities for schools to create a positive and thriving culture.

Practical ways to bring PERMA into your school environment

The suggestions here are designed to be woven into your school practices; you can cherry pick from them as required. They can simply become part of a resource kit to use when needing additional ideas to maintain your momentum.

Practical strategies to bring positive emotions such as joy, gratitude and hope:

- **Celebrate:** Create opportunities to celebrate accomplishments of the staff and students through meetings, assemblies, newsletters, shout-outs or walls of gratitude that are displayed in classrooms or common spaces.
- **Gratitude:** Make the practice of gratitude, where students and staff reflect on what they are thankful for, a common event. Have students reflect at the end of each day so they leave school with a positive at the front of mind.
- **Kindness:** Create opportunities for acts of kindness to encourage students and staff to share positive experiences. Remind staff and students that kindness matters when no one is looking!
- **Shout-out walls:** Create a display where students and staff can write notes recognising positive moments or people who have brightened their day.
- **Mindfulness:** Schedule times to pause and be mindful during the school day. Use some of the activities discussed earlier in this book.
- **Gratitude journals:** Give students and staff journals where they can note daily positive experiences or moments of gratitude. This can help cultivate optimism and positive outlooks.

Practical strategies to bring about engagement and flow into your school:

- **Tailor learning:** Use the strengths of students and staff to drive lesson planning and initiatives. Strength-based education can help increase engagement.
- **Project-based learning:** Provide project-based learning opportunities where students can dive deeply into subjects they're passionate about with a hands-on approach.
- **Passion projects:** As an extension of project-based learning, provide students opportunities to choose something personal to explore deeply in a passion project. This increases autonomy and engagement.

- **Co-curricular activities:** Offer a wide variety of activities outside the classroom that cater to different interests (such as sports, arts, STEM clubs, cultural activities and so on). Attempt to find something for all students to engage them beyond the school-based curriculum.
- **Learning hubs:** Set up hubs in classrooms where students can explore big questions to develop understanding at their own pace. This caters for different learning styles, increases engagement through self-directed learning and promotes the 'teacher as facilitator' model, allowing students to drive the learning process through inquiry and problem-solving rather than direct instruction.

Practical strategies to create strong, healthy and positive relationships in the school community:

- **Mentoring/buddies:** Create mentoring programs that encourage positive, supportive relationships. Have staff mentor newer colleagues and older students mentor younger ones.
- **Community:** Find ways to bring the community together through events such as family nights, picnics, concerts, quiz nights or team-building activities that bring everyone from the community together.
- **Circle time:** Create opportunities for circle time, having students and staff check in with each other. This helps develop empathy and understanding, ultimately establishing stronger relationships.
- **Collaboration:** Structure times where teachers are able to work with each other through a co-teaching program or in a professional learning community. This helps develop a supportive environment where professional bonds can be strengthened.

Practical strategies to help staff and students find purpose and to connect with something bigger than themselves:

- **Vision and mission:** Make sure that your vision and mission statements are obvious, clear and regularly communicated so students and staff understand how they contribute to this larger purpose.
- **Service:** Weave opportunities for service into the curriculum, for students to understand that what they are doing has an impact on the wider community.
- **Reflect:** Reflecting on your values and goals and how they align with the school can create a stronger sense of purpose. Practised regularly, it keeps front of mind how your work contributes to the greater good of the school and the students.

- **Culture:** Cultural diversity within your environment should be celebrated. Provide opportunities for students to share their cultural background through different means (such as presentations, food and performances). This fosters a sense of inclusion, belonging and respect. A student-lead Inclusivity Committee will also add agency to driving an agenda of inclusion.
- **Guest speakers:** Bringing people in to the school community to share their joy, passion and experiences for what they do/have achieved helps illustrate how we can find meaning and purpose in our studies or chosen fields.
- **Legacy:** Explain to the students that we should always aim to leave a place better than we found it. In our school environment, this would be our legacy to those who follow. Have students identify projects that will leave a positive impact on the school for years to come. For example, a garden project or beautifying an area.

Practical strategies to help create a culture of accomplishment to help staff and students find success:

- **Goals:** Make goal-setting part of school life for staff and students: SMART (specific, measurable, achievable, relevant, time-bound) or WOOP (wish, outcome, obstacle, plan) goals can be used to regularly reflect on progress.
- **Mindset:** Explore the different mindsets that people can have, promoting a growth mindset as one that rewards effort, builds resilience and increases persistence. Challenges, conflicts and mistakes should be seen as opportunities for learning and growth.
- **Recognition:** Build opportunities to celebrate staff and student accomplishments by highlighting them in meaningful ways. Understand that recognition can mean different things to different people. Find what works for your staff and students.
- **Personal portfolios:** Have a portfolio for students to track and reflect on their accomplishments (these can be linked to learning and wellbeing intentions as well as personal goals). Making this a regular feature of the week creates evidence of growth and accomplishments that students can look back on with pride.

Hope and wellbeing

When it comes down to it, it is hope that keeps us going – be it in our personal or professional lives. Hope, to be able to pursue our goals with focus and commitment; hope, that helps us carry on through challenging times; and hope, that works as a force to take us beyond wishful thinking. Through all of the chapters in this book, hope is a repetitive theme. How do we foster a culture of wellbeing and a desire to create resilient, flourishing humans without hope?

What is hope?

Our common belief is that hope is our ability that we will be able to discover ways of achieving our goals and maintain the motivation to pursue them. According to psychologist Charles Snyder's hope theory (2022), there are two main components that are essential: agency and pathways. That is, having grit to pursue your goals and strategies to help you achieve them.

This book has discussed the role meaning and purpose plays in our wellbeing. Hope is a vital component of this. How are we able to see a brighter future for ourselves without hope?

Hope requires a conscious effort and a focus on the future. It enables us to find a positive, even when facing challenges. It can be as simple as telling yourself that bad times don't last forever. By maintaining hope, we can become more resilient, have a more positive perspective on life and reduce the levels of anxiety and stress we may feel. This can be due to the increased levels of optimism we experience, ultimately reducing our feelings of hopelessness.

Research has indicated that students who have a 'hopeful outlook' develop higher levels of resilience and increased persistence when challenged academically. The ability to project a positive future, despite these challenges, helps maintain their desire, focus and grit to work towards their goals. They learn to see that these challenges are opportunities, and through problem-solving or being solutions-focused, they can avoid becoming frustrated. This is equally as important for teachers who need to remain hopeful to maintain commitment and motivation to cope with the many competing demands of the profession.

As discussed earlier, school settings that promote optimism, goal-setting and future-oriented thinking are ones that have hope embedded into their school culture.

Hope can be embedded into school culture through the following activities:

- Regular opportunities for students to set realistic and meaningful goals. Use SMART or WOOP goals for students to learn to break down large goals into smaller, manageable tasks.
- Create visual aids such as charts or personal planners for students to track their goals and progress.
- Make problem-solving exercises, based on real-world scenarios, an integral component of daily activities or as part of project work. Explore multiple solutions to the problems so students can see that often there is more than one way to solve issues.
- Create a vision board and a progress wall where students can display visual representations of their goals and record their accomplishments.
- Make progress a focus by celebrating small achievements along the way, helping students maintain motivation and hope to achieve their goals.
- Use language representative of a growth mindset to reinforce that skills, abilities and understanding can be developed over time.

As professionals we are dedicated to creating an environment where all members of our community can thrive. Having hope as a central component of our school culture, we set about providing an environment that cultivates a love of learning and a strong sense of wellbeing, by equipping them with all the skills they need to face conflict or uncertainty in life.

Keeping hope central to your strategic and wellbeing plans will mean that the blueprint provided in this book – developing a common language; starting with the staff; maintaining a focus on yourself; developing resilience, agency, social and emotional capacity; developing a whole-school approach; and focusing on the practices of wellbeing – will provide you, your staff and your students the tools they need to navigate life's ups and downs. You can all look forward to a more hopeful tomorrow.

Afterword
UNLOCKING THE PATH TO WELLBEING

As we reach the end of this book, take a moment to reflect on the journey we've taken through these chapters. We've explored the concept of wellbeing – that it is not just a buzzword or a fleeting initiative, but rather a deeper commitment to fostering environments where students and staff are afforded the opportunities to thrive. It is about equipping individuals with the skills to navigate life's challenges, building resilience, and creating school cultures that prioritise growth, connection and purpose.

At its core, wellbeing is not about finding happiness but about having resilience, flexibility and adaptability. It requires understanding of the unique context of your school and ensuring that any initiatives will be of benefit to everyone – students, staff and families. Resilience, both for educators and students, is essential, but it is important to clarify that it is not about pushing through at all costs. It is about building capacity to recover, adapt and grow; it is the ability to bounce back from adversity.

Shared understanding is key. Defining commonly used terms in your context – for example, 'emotional literacy' and 'character strengths' – creates a common language that supports a cohesive school culture. Trust and connection are equally critical; when staff feel valued and supported, they are better equipped to inspire and guide their students. Purpose, for both educators and students, drives wellbeing, while forgiveness helps clear the way for continued growth.

A whole-school approach embeds wellbeing into the culture, making it an everyday practice and forming habits rather than an add on. Whether it is integrating gratitude, fostering student agency or creating trauma-informed classrooms, these strategies create safe, inclusive spaces where everyone can flourish. To ensure longevity, aligning wellbeing with existing frameworks and maintaining a focus on shared goals helps embed this work into the fabric of the school.

This book is not the end of the story – it is an invitation to begin, or continue, your own wellbeing journey. Each small step, whether as an educator, leader or member of the school community, contributes to creating spaces where everyone can flourish. Reflect on your context, take bold actions and lead with purpose. Together, we can reimagine what's possible and transform our schools into places of hope, growth and thriving for all.

RESOURCES

Frameworks

Australian Student Wellbeing Framework (ASWF)	Guiding principles for safety, inclusivity and social-emotional development across school communities.
Visible Wellbeing	Strength-based approaches, emotional literacy and teaching tools for wellbeing integration.
Be You	A framework for educators to promote mental health through professional learning and resources.
Friendly Schools	Evidence-based strategies for creating supportive school environments and fostering positive relationships.

Programs

Zones of Regulation	Tools to identify and regulate emotions, creating a common language for self-regulation.
URSTRONG	Empowering students to create healthy friendships, conflict resolution strategies and communication skills.
Kimochis	Engaging tools such as plush characters to teach feelings, communication and empathy.

Growing with Gratitude	Activities to develop a positive mindset, gratitude and resilience in daily life.
The PEACE Pack	Evidence-based program focusing on reducing bullying through peer support, teacher training and whole-school approaches.
You Can Do It! Education	Five keys to success: confidence, persistence, organisation, getting along and emotional resilience.
Aussie Optimism	Promotes optimism, resilience and positive mental health through evidence-based curriculum resources.
Confident Kids	Programs to develop self-esteem, social skills and resilience in a small group or classroom setting.
Grow Your Mind	Resources to teach mindfulness, self-regulation and emotional literacy through playful tools and stories.
Peaceful Kids	Programs to reduce anxiety and stress through mindfulness and relaxation practices.
The Resilience Project	Curriculum integration, presentations, journalling and mindfulness activities.
Bounce Back!	SEL skills, coping strategies and resilience-building through storybooks and lesson plans.
MindUP	Brain-focused lessons, mindfulness practices and gratitude-based activities.
Smiling Mind Education	App-based guided meditations, curriculum resources for mindfulness in the classroom.
Positive Education Program	Whole-school implementation of PERMAH (positive emotions, engagement, relationships, meaning, achievement, health).

PATHS (Promoting Alternative Thinking Strategies)	Lessons on self-control, problem-solving and interpersonal relationships.
Friends Resilience	Evidence-based practices to manage anxiety, develop coping strategies and foster resilience.
Personal Well-Being Lessons (Ilona Boniwell)	Practical wellbeing activities, goal-setting, resilience-building and strengths-focused interventions.
Second Step	Lessons on empathy, problem-solving, self-regulation and bullying prevention.
Mind Matters	Focuses on mental health awareness, building resilience and emotional wellbeing for teenagers.

REFERENCES

American Psychological Association. (2019). *The road to resilience.* www.apa.org/helpcenter/road-resilience

Barr, S. (2024). *Educate to self-regulate: Empowering learners for lifelong success.* Amba Press.

Batson, C. D. (2011). *Altruism in humans.* Oxford University Press.

Borgonovi, F., & Pál, J. (2016). *A framework for the analysis of student wellbeing in the PISA 2015 study: Being 15 in 2015* (OECD Education Working Papers No. 140). OECD Publishing.

Brown, B. (2018). *Dare to lead: Brave work. Tough conversations. Whole hearts.* Random House.

Cross, D., & Lester, L. (2023). *Leading improvement in school community wellbeing.* ACER Press

Department for Education. (n.d.). *Wellbeing for Learning and Life framework.* Government of South Australia.

Department of Education. (n.d.). *Wellbeing framework for schools.* New South Wales Government.

Department of Education. (n.d.). *Student learning and wellbeing framework.* Queensland Government.

Department of Education and Training. (n.d.). *Vision for learning and wellbeing.* State Government of Victoria.

Duckworth, A. L., Peterson, C., Matthews, M. D., & Kelly, D. R. (2007). Grit: Perseverance and passion for long-term goals. *Journal of Personality and Social Psychology, 92*(6), 1087–1101.

Duckworth, A. L., & Quinn, P. D. (2009). Development and validation of the Short Grit Scale (Grit-S). *Journal of Personality Assessment, 91*(2), 166–174.

Duckworth, A. (2017). G*rit: The power of passion and perseverance.* Scribner.

Dweck, C. S. (2006). *Mindset: The new psychology of success.* Random House.

Emmons, R. A. (2007). *Thanks!: How the new science of gratitude can make you happier.* Houghton Mifflin Harcourt.

Foote, N. (Host). (2024, August). *Enhancing future skills with game-based learning | Empowering students in STEAM* (Season 3, Episode 1) [Audio podcast episode]. In *The Jigsaw24 EdTech Podcast*. Jigsaw24.

Fredrickson, B. L. (2009). *Positivity: Top-notch research reveals the 3-to-1 ratio that will change your life*. Crown.

Gable, S. L., Reis, H. T., Impett, E. A., & Asher, E. R. (2004). What do you do when things go right? The intrapersonal and interpersonal benefits of sharing positive events. *Journal of Personality and Social Psychology*, 87(2), 228.

Gillham, J., Reivich, K., Freres, D. R., Chaplin, T. M., Shatté, A. J., Samuels, B., Elkon, A. G. L., Litzinger, S., Lascher, M., Gallop, R., & Seligman, M. E. P. (2007). School-based prevention of depressive symptoms: A randomized controlled study of the effectiveness and specificity of the Penn Resiliency Program. *Journal of Consulting and Clinical Psychology*, 75(1), 9–19.

Kellerman, G. R., & Seligman, M. E. P. (2023). *TomorrowMind: Thriving at work with resilience, creativity, and connection – now and in an uncertain future*. Atria Books.

Kerford, D. (2018, October). *Why your kids don't need to be friends with everybody!* Sydney Morning Herald. Written by K. Edwards.

Manuel, A. (2022). *Growing with gratitude: Building resilience, happiness, and mental wellbeing in our schools and homes*. Wiley.

McLean, S. (2018). *Sexts, texts and selfies: How to keep your children safe in the digital space* (Rev. ed.). Penguin Random House Australia.

Miller, C. A., & Frisch, M. B. (2009). *Creating your best life: The ultimate life list guide*. Sterling Publishing.

Miller, C. A. (2017). *Getting grit: The evidence-based approach to cultivating passion, perseverance, and purpose*. Sounds True.

Mills, P. J., Redwine, L., Wilson, K., & Pung, M. A. (2015, April 9). *The grateful heart: The role of gratitude in health and well-being*. American Psychological Association. www.apa.org/news/press/releases/2015/04/grateful-heart

Nawana Parker, M. (2020). *The resilience and wellbeing toolbox: Building character and competence through life's ups and downs*. Routledge.

Niemiec, R. M., & McGrath, R. E. (2019). *The power of character strengths: Appreciate and ignite your positive personality*. VIA Institute on Character.

Quinlan, D. M., & Hone, L. C. (2020). *The educators' guide to whole-school wellbeing: A practical guide to getting started, best-practice process, and effective implementation*. Routledge.

Reivich, K., & Shatté, A. (2003). *The resilience factor: 7 keys to finding your inner strength and overcoming life's hurdles*. Broadway Books.

Seligman, M. E. P., & Csikszentmihalyi, M. (2000). Positive psychology: An introduction. *American Psychologist,* 55(1), 5–14.

Seligman, M. E. P., Steen, T. A., Park, N., & Peterson, C. (2005). Positive psychology progress: Empirical validation of interventions. *American Psychologist, 60*(5), 410-421. https://doi.org/10.1037/0003-066X.60.5.410

Seligman, M. E. P. (2011). *Flourish: A visionary new understanding of happiness and well-being.* Free Press.

Street, H. (2018). *Contextual wellbeing: Creating positive schools from the inside out.* Wise Solutions.

Snyder, C. R. (2002). Hope theory: Rainbows in the mind. *Psychological Inquiry, 13*(4), 249-275.

van Cuylenburg, H. (2020). *The resilience project: Finding happiness through gratitude, empathy & mindfulness.* Penguin Random House.

Waters, L. (2017). *The strength switch: How the new science of strength-based parenting can help your child and your teen to flourish.* Avery.

Waters, L. (2015). Strength-Based Parenting and Life Satisfaction in Teenagers. *Advances in Social Sciences Research Journal, 2,* 158-173.

Waters, L. (2021). Positive education pedagogy: Shifting teacher mindsets, practice, and language to make wellbeing visible in classrooms. In M. L. Kern & M. L. Wehmeyer (Eds.), *The Palgrave handbook of positive education* (pp. 127-147). Palgrave Macmillan.

White, M. A., & Waters, L. E. (2015). A case study of 'The Good School:' Examples of the use of Peterson's strengths-based approach with students. *Journal of Positive Psychology, 10*(1), 69-76

White, M. A., & Murray, A. S. (2015). Building a positive institution. In: White, M., Murray, A. (eds) *Evidence-Based Approaches in Positive Education.* Positive Education. Springer.

Yeager, D. S., Romero, C., Paunesku, D., Hulleman, C. S., Schneider, B., Hinojosa, C., Lee, H. Y., O'Brien, J., Flint, K., Roberts, A., Trott, J., Greene, D., Walton, G. M., & Dweck, C. S. (2016). Using design thinking to improve psychological interventions: The case of the growth mindset during the transition to high school. *Journal of Educational Psychology, 108*(3), 374-391.

ACKNOWLEDGEMENTS

For many years people have told me that I should write a book. I guess the timing just wasn't quite right until now. But I didn't get here on my own. There are so many people I need to thank who have helped me on my professional and personal journey:

- Simon Murray, Mathew White and David Hine gave me the opportunity, guidance and support to grow my skills and understanding in wellbeing. In addition, the leadership teams at both Trinity and St Peter's have supported and encouraged me to pursue my passion for wellbeing.

- Karen Reivich and the Penn Resiliency Team provided a transformative professional development opportunity that deepened my understanding of resilience as a practical skill that can be taught, modelled and applied in real-life contexts.

- Professor Martin Seligman and Dr Michael Carr-Gregg were pivotal in shaping my initial thoughts and behaviour change.

- Professor Lea Waters has been, and continues to be, a beacon of light for me with her work in positive psychology. Her focus on identifying and cultivating the best versions of ourselves has revolutionised the way I think about personal growth and flourishing.

- Helen Street's expertise in developmental psychology has brought a whole new dimension to my understanding of wellbeing.

- Dana Kerford's work with URSTRONG has helped me explore the importance of relationships in student wellbeing.

- Madhavi Nawana Parker has offered invaluable insights into supporting young people's mental health.

- Ash Manuel's Growing with Gratitude program has provided a fresh perspective on cultivating gratitude and mindfulness as everyday habits.
- Toni Noble's contributions to social-emotional learning (SEL) have shaped my understanding of the importance of emotional intelligence.
- Donna Cross's insights through her research on student health and safety have been a source of inspiration for me – giving greater understanding of preventative measures in creating safe, supportive environments in schools and communities.
- Carolyn Adams Miller's work on grit and goal-setting has deepened my understanding of cultivating perseverance and passion for long-term goals.

I have been fortunate to work with these incredible professionals who have helped establish my beliefs, understandings and practices regarding how to create thriving students and environments. Their collective influence has helped me link the science of learning with the science of wellbeing, showing me how these two areas intersect and complement one another. This perspective has clarified what's possible when wellbeing is prioritised in schools. These individuals have deepened my understanding and equipped me with the tools to approach wellbeing with empathy and creativity. I am truly grateful for their influence.

My gratitude extends further to Professor Lea Waters, Madhavi Nawana Parker, Ash Manuel, Christopher Clausen and Richard Love who provided valuable insights in the development of this book. I thank them for their honesty, integrity and feedback.

Finally, I need to thank my family who have all been with me on this journey. It has not always been smooth sailing, and I wish I could say that I was always able to practice what I preach – but as you read in the book, I have needed to practice forgiveness of myself for any mistakes I have made along the way. None of us are perfect – either as educators or parents, and I am far from it!

Throughout this book, I hope the recurring theme of gratitude has been obvious. My sincerest appreciation goes to all of those mentioned above. Their insights continue to inspire me to prioritise wellbeing as a core foundation helping our communities to work towards thriving together.

ABOUT THE AUTHOR

David Kolpak is well-known for his work in wellbeing education. Since 2012, Kolpak has been developing initiatives and creating programs to help teachers and students bring out the best in young people.

As an educator for over 30 years, Kolpak has had opportunities to work in various roles to help develop his understanding of the whole child. As a former class teacher, Head of House, Curriculum Coordinator, Deputy Principal and now Principal, Kolpak works to bring all facets of education together to develop an understanding that wellbeing (for staff and students) must be the foundation for all schools if they want to provide a thriving culture.

As a Principal, Kolpak knows first-hand the changing nature of the school environment. With the increasing demands and the changing landscape on student wellbeing, his work on educator wellbeing is becoming increasingly important. Kolpak helps frame positive starting points to school staff to be the best version of themselves in order to bring out the best in the students.

Kolpak lives in Adelaide with his wife and three children, and is the first to admit that he hasn't always put into practice what he speaks about. He reminds us that, as humans, even with the very best intentions, we are going to make mistakes – hence his belief in the power of forgiveness in a wellbeing framework.

www.ingramcontent.com/pod-product-compliance
Lightning Source LLC
Chambersburg PA
CBHW050358120526
44590CB00015B/1736